BEHOLD

I GIVE UNTO YOU

POWER

This Book is Presented to

_____

by

_____

Comments

_____

Date: _____   Time: _____

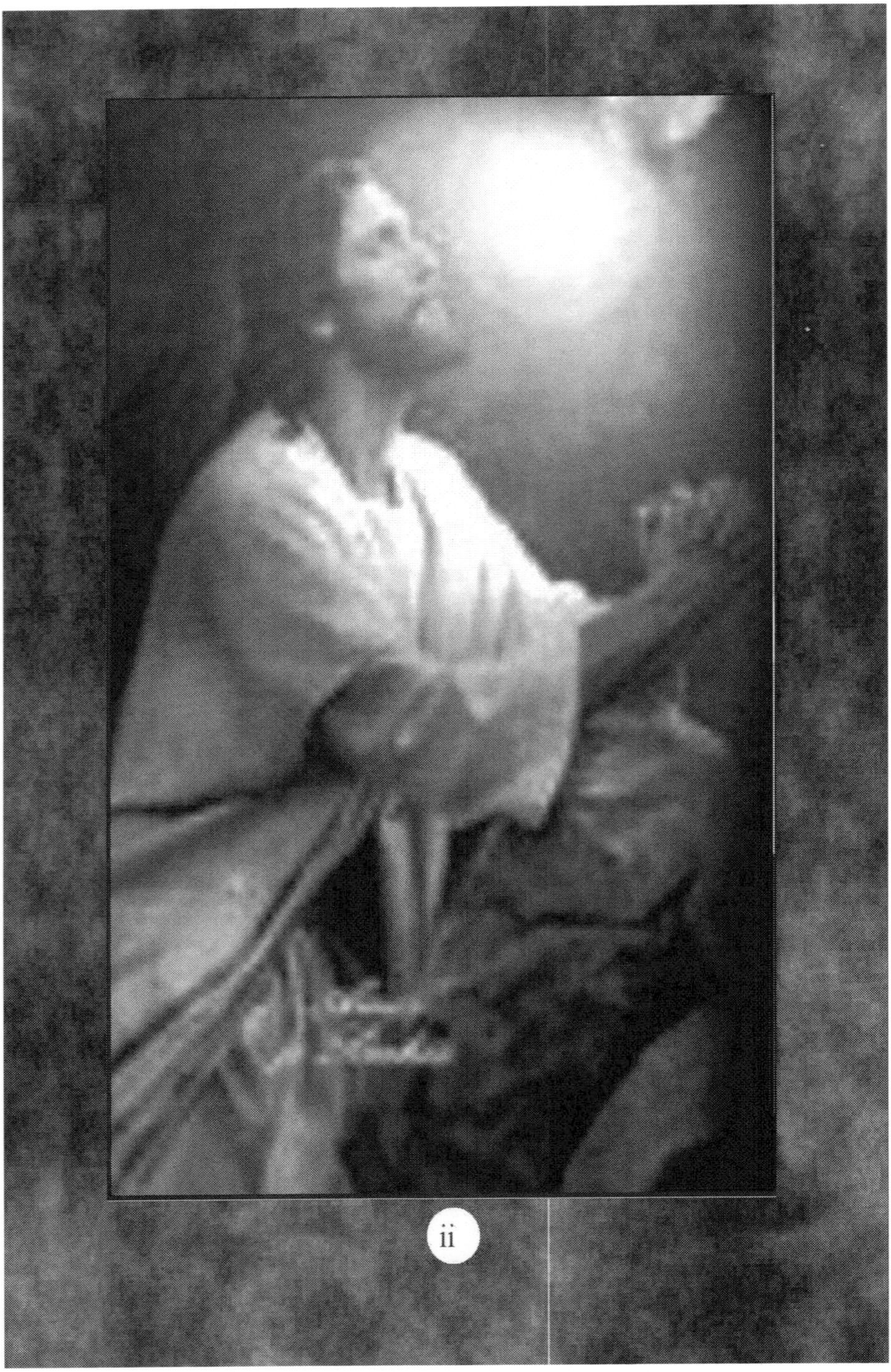

BEHOLD I GIVE UNTO YOU POWER

-IYKE NATHAN UZORMA

Harbinger Books.
P. O.Box 1562 Effurun, Warri, Nigeria.
Email: harbinger_nig@yahoo.com

Copyright © 2012 by Iyke Nathan Uzorma.

ISBN: Softcover   978-1-4797-1830-6
       Ebook   978-1-4797-1831-3

All rights reserved. No part of this book may be reproduced or transmitted in any form or by any means, electronic or mechanical, including photocopying, recording, or by any information storage and retrieval system, without permission in writing from the copyright owner.

This book was printed in the United States of America.

To order additional copies of this book, contact:
Xlibris Corporation
1-888-795-4274
www.Xlibris.com
Orders@Xlibris.com
122492

DEDICATED To the HOLY SPIRIT

By Whom

This Work Is Done

CLARIFICATION OF IDENTITY
(Iyke Nathan Uzorma is not Protus Nathan Uzorma)

Following the column of Prof. Protus Nathan Uzorma (Nathan Uzorma Protus) on **'Philosophical Reflections'** every Wednesday in the 'DAILY SUN' newspaper (Nigeria), several people at one time or the other, have genuinely sought to know from us whether **Prof. Iyke Nathan Uzorma, Harbinger of the Last Covenant,** *(of the former Occult Grand Master, Now in Christ fame)* is the one writing **'Philosophical Reflections'** in the 'DAILY SUN.'

Some people, however, having mistaken Protus Nathan Uzorma to be Iyke Nathan Uzorma, have cast aspersions on the latter based on the writings of the former. For instance, one Onyero Mgbejum in an article posted in the website (www.sunnewsonline.com., **'The question of virgin birth and the deity of Jesus,'** Thursday April 16, 2009), judged and condemned the **Harbinger of the Last Covenant** (IYKE NATHAN UZORMA) while reacting to the article of Protus Nathan Uzorma. Part of what Onyero Mgbejum wrote, reads:

> "I read with keen interest and inclination towards asking searching questions, the articles written in your widely read Daily Sun newspaper of Wednesday, March 18, 2009. In the two articles written by Sina Adedipe

and Prof. Nathan Uzorma Protus, the questions of Virgin Birth and Deity of Our Lord and Saviour Jesus Christ are subjects of comment by the two writers. In his article Prof. Uzorma said that **'the great question to the Christian world is: Why is the virgin birth of other star beings and sages said to be demonic and that of Christ divine'**.... Things of the Spirit can only be perceived by those who have the Spirit of God, those who have accepted the Lordship of the Lord Jesus Christ. People like **Prof. Iyke Nathan Uzorma**... is deceptive and thus should be regarded as an antichrist... **Prof. Iyke** should also be regarded as an atheist empowered by Satan to confuse and deceive people."

While we pray the LORD to forgive Onyero Mgbejum for this malicious error, including those who falsely allege that Iyke Nathan Uzorma has gone back to the occult and for whatever the powers of darkness have used same to achieve, we also advice anyone who claims to 'defend' the LORD to be very watchful through the Holy Spirit, so that one will not degrade the true work of Christ while 'fighting' for the Almighty. And for the avoidance of doubt, let it be known that Prof. Iyke Nathan Uzorma is the elder brother of Prof. Protus

Behold I give unto you power

Nathan Uzorma. Both are different persons from the same parents. While 'Nathan' is the family middle name, 'Uzorma' is the family surname.

Remain blessed!

Signed:

MRS. EME EKANEM ETUK, M.A.
Special Assistant, Outreach Affairs, To The
HARBINGER OF THE LAST COVENANT

IYKE NATHAN UZORMA

PROTUS NATHAN UZORMA

COMMENTS ON THE MISSION AND PUBLICATIONS OF
IYKE NATHAN UZORMA

"It is indeed a miracle that Prof. Iyke Nathan Uzorma, a well known Guru and Perfect Master of Esoteric Mysteries...has been humbled and convicted by the Holy Spirit to acknowledge and accept the sovereignty of the true Christ over his life."
-PROF. OLADEJO OKEDIJI
Former Dean, Faculty of Social Sciences, University of Lagos, Nigeria.

"Though several publications on religious and spiritual matters exist, but from my personal experience, none the world over is as authoritative as the works of Prof. Iyke Nathan Uzorma, Harbinger of the Last Covenant."
-HIS EXCELLENCY,
YURI KWAKU BAAWINE
Former Ambassador of Ghana in Saudi Arabia.

"My meeting Prof. Iyke Nathan Uzorma, Harbinger of the Last Covenant, in Nigeria, greatly lifted my spirit and opened my eyes more on a deeper aspect of the mysteries of life."
-PROF. YOSIAH MAGEMBE BWATWA
Dean, Faculty of Education, Tumaini University, Dar-es-Salaam, Tanzania.

Behold I give unto you power

"We thank God for using in our day and age His Harbinger, Prof. Iyke, to open the eyes of many in his spiritual mission that is divinely bound to move the world"
-CHIEF DONALD UGBAJA, NPM, mni
Deputy Inspector General of Police (rtd.), Abuja, Nigeria

"The Harbinger of the Last Covenant, who was former Occult Grand Master, appears plain and ordinary but, as revealed to me, he is a head lion in the pride of God's lions."
-PROPHETESS NNEKA A. UDI-KEN
Founder, Tabitha (Mercy) Prayer Ministry, Effurun, Warri, Nigeria.

"My respected mentor, Prof. (Apostle) Iyke Nathan Uzorma, Harbinger of the Last Covenant, thanks for teaching me the reality of the forces of darkness, their manipulations and weaknesses. Thank you sir and may God continue to use you to bless our generation."
-MOSES AYEKETA
Presiding Bishop, House of Prayer, Christ Restoration Centre, Tulsa, Ok., USA.

"Dear Iyke Nathan Uzorma, after reading your books, I experienced a fresh and new anointing upon my life."
-PASTOR HAYFORD A. B.
Assemblies of God Church
P.O. Box 95422, Tel Aviv, Israel.

"Your books completely changed my weakness in spirit. To be precise, I was a Muslim and converted into the Christian Religion and got salvation through Christ."
-PRINCE HABIB WINFUL
Harter Str. 69 Graz-8053
Austria, West Europe.

"Man of God, I thank God for your book which helped to strengthen me in the Power of Jesus Christ."
-NATHAN C. U.
26 Friedrich Ebert Street,
57-518 Betzdorf, Germany.

"I read your book and the blessing I got from it is beyond what I can express.
-DAVIDSON O.
Don Whari 445-2 Kyonggid 0445-890
Seoul, South Korea.

"I must say that your book is an overall experience compared to others whose testimonies we've read."
-REV'D. C.S.D. OSUIGWE
Onitsha District H.Q.
The Apostolic Church of Nigeria.

"Your book has strengthened me in my Christian life. I am now anxious to read other books by you."
-RICHARD REMNARINE
Plot 8, Springlands Corriverton Berbice,
Guyana, South America.

Behold I give unto you power

"Words are inadequate for me to express the contents of your books. I thank God for the enlightenment you have given us."
-REV'D. ROBERT ARYIKEN
29, Rosemead Ave,, Mitcham Surrey
CR4 IEZ England, United Kingdom.

"I came across your book and could not put it aside but had to finish it in hours. I thank God so much for your life."
-PROF. P.A.DUAH
University of Ghana, Legon, Accra.

"Your books have changed my life and the lives of friends and families."
-W.P. LIESCHING
P.O.Box 2334, White River 1240, South Africa.

"The books of Prof. Iyke Uzorma, Harbinger of the Last Covenant, are nobel and highly enriching to humanity."
-PROF. SMART O. NWAOKORO
Head, Dept. Of Animal Science,
University of Benin, Nigeria

CONTENTS

Clarification of Identity.................................vi
Comments..ix
Acknowledgment..xv
Foreword...xvi
Preface To This Edition................................xviii
Introduction.. xx

CHAPTERS:

1. **My Letter To The Reader**..........................*25*
   *The Power You Seek *The Spirit Is Power
   *Man: The Power Unit *Manifesting
   Power *Power Beyond The Surface
   *Our Lord Jesus Christ

2. **Diverse Power**..*43*
   *Three Major Aspects Of Power
   *Recognition Of Your Level Of Power
   *Physical Power *Metaphysical Power

3. **The Highest Power**.....................................*64*
   *Esoteric Versus Spiritual *Encounter
   Of Powers *Duplication Of Spiritual
   Power *Limitation Of Bogus Powers
   *The Master Key

4. **Power For Victory**......................................*77*
   *Serpents And Scorpions *The Power
   Of Victory *Restoration Of Work
   *How God Speaks To Me *Invisible Warfare

Behold I give unto you power

5. **Stronghold Of True Power**.........................*90*
    *The Power Of Unity *Knowing The Truth
    *Marriage Restoration Via His Power
    *Channels Of His Power

6. **Bona-fide Channel Of Power**....................*106*
    *The Banner Of Victory *Better Understanding
    *Spiritual Lesson *The Final Order

7. **The High Craft Of Darkness**....................*118*
    *Why Some Shepherds Lack Power
    *Title Vis-À-Vis Power *His Seal And
    Recognition Of Power *The Blood Of
    Jesus Christ *Man Made Path

8. **All Things Are Possible**.............................*136*
    *Beyond Limitation *Revealer Of Secrets
    *Power In Confession *Restoration Power

9. **Signs And Signet Of Power**......................*149*
    *A New Beginning *The Reality Of God's Power
    *Operations Of His Power *Divine Provision

10. **How To Be Firm In Power**........................*163*
    *Faith And Constant Prayer *Meditate On
    God's Word

11. **Books By Iyke Nathan Uzorma**...............*171*

ACKNOWLEDGMENT

*I*am sincerely indebted to all those who have encouraged me in one way or the other in my divine mandate in Christ. They are channels through which the Holy Spirit made it easy for me to partake, in my own little way, in the great move of His Divine Power towards the spiritual liberation of humans.

I am also indebted to all the lovers of my mission on the path of Light, in different parts of the world. Their calls, mails, testimonies and prayers are enough for me to praise God that truly in Him our labour is not in vain.

Special thanks to my wife, Lady Udeme Nathan Uzorma, as well as my Personal Assistant, Michael Isemin and Chris Akunesi, for their editorial work, including Churkylove, for the cover design.

- Iyke Nathan Uzorma

FOREWORD

The book now with you - BEHOLD I GIVE UNTO YOU POWER, is an indepth treatise that expounds from mundane through far-flung concepts of spiritual and metaphysical powers in the Universe. Confounding, perplexing, profound and chilling in exposition and presentation, the work is an eye-opener and a spiritual must read for the faithful and the faithless - the various minds that make up our world.

The author writes with the greatest conviction as directed under the hands of the Holy Spirit. Aside from the personal experiences at his disposal, the graphic expositions and sequence of all narratives in his writings have the solid Scriptural backing that further confirms the guidance of the Spirit of God.

It is clearly evident that the works of Prof. Iyke Nathan Uzorma are a compendium of vast plethora showing narration, exposition and transparent pictures of his spiritual warfare treatise all rolled in one. As he writes, the words appear to talk and explain in pictures not the reader's mind parse but that of the Lord at work.

The message in this book, BEHOLD I GIVE UNTO YOU POWER, stretches from now to the next generation and beyond. Therefore we thank God for using in our day and age His HARBINGER, Prof. Iyke, to open the eyes of many in his spiritual mission that is divinely bound to move the world.

I am confident that this book will uplift the spiritual life of those who will faithfully read, appropriate and apply the great message contained in it, as it has done for me, to the praise and glory of our Heavenly Father, in the mighty name of our Lord Jesus Christ - Amen.

CHIEF DONALD UGBAJA, *NPM, mni*
Deputy Inspector General of
Police (rtd.), Abuja, Nigeria.

Behold I give unto you power

PREFACE TO THIS EDITION

I wrote the first edition of this book, Behold I Give Unto You Power, between November to December, 1998, and it was published in January 1999. The format of that edition has now changed. The present 'Revised and Enlarged Edition' has ten chapters. New works are added to this edition.

The first chapter is designed to guide the reader on the path of discovering the Divine Power within man over all the powers of darkness. The nature of the Higher Aspect of man and the radiation of the Holy Spirit, as well as the Highest Power which is Jesus Christ, are also explained. The second chapter deals with powers on both the physical and metaphysical levels. The third chapter shows the sole ultimate Power above other levels of power with practical evidence.

This book holds that the Power which Christ gave us to tread on serpent and scorpions is the Power above powers. Chapters four to ten are questions and answers on the subject matter of the Words of Our Lord Jesus Christ thus "Behold I Give Unto you Power", being the title of this treatise. These questions came from my very close associates during our fasting and prayer programme, upon the conception of the title of this book. They cover diverse aspects, such as what 'serpents and scorpions' are, the Power of daily victory, the nature of spiritual warfare, the essence of unity, how to serve as

Preface to this edition

the human channel of true Power, the high crafts of the powers of darkness, why some shepherds lack the highest Power of God in our time, and much more.

I do hope that the reader of this book will become more established in THAT Power which is above all powers through this work. So be it. Amen!

- Iyke Nathan Uzorma

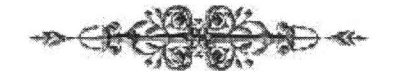

INTRODUCTION

"Behold, I give unto you power to tread on serpents and scorpions, and over all the power of the enemy: and nothing shall by any means hurt you"
— Luke 10 : 19.

It is under the direct influence of the Holy Spirit that I write to you on the practical aspect of the Supreme Power of the Multidimensional God, as may be demonstrated in the world of man. And let me inform you from the onset that the Scripture text of this treatise is taken from the Words of our Lord as recorded in **LUKE chapter 10 verse 19**.

The Power of God is real! In this book the reality of the Highest Power is evident from diverse channels including my personal experience. When you directly experience the true Power of the Godhead in the Highest essence of the perfection of the Blood of Jesus Christ, you will know most truly that Christ is REAL and ABSOLUTE.

Now, remember that the phrase *"serpents and scorpions"* used by the Lord **(in Luke 10: 19)**, has to do with the multitudinous network or empire of the vicious Astral powers of darkness. These include demonic entities, mephistophelian psychic powers, elements and all paraphernalia of darkness, mighty warriors of the

Introduction

dark world, black magicians, masters and grandmasters of the vicious occult and esoteric systems, witches and wizards, necromancers, amongst others.

The aforementioned was the framework in which my past life revolved. Thus I was highly involved in diverse related operations of the powers of darkness both within and beyond the cycle of the grandmasters, which hold the most vicious power known as' serpents and scorpions'. To this end, when I speak to the earthman, that he should be strong in the Lord to have victory over the empire of the forces of darkness, I speak solely because I was with them.

Thus be informed that the entire operation of the powers of darkness (serpents and scorpions), which include their human agents, is to manipulate and subjugate humans in diverse ways. From my past involvement in that system, however, I can state categorically that the operation of the proclaimed 'serpents and scorpions' works mainly on those whose lives have not risen beyond the mundane. I mean those whose lives are not yet lifted by the Eternal Light of Christ.

Generally speaking, however, the vicious Astral entities could rise against a marriage so as to dominate it. They could rise against one's promotion in an establishment. They could rise against one's finance to make one not to excel. They could rise against one with sickness, lack of favor, serious court case; fatal accident, even with death and other related predicaments. They could also rise against a believer, who is not watchful, and cause him to be slothful, spiritually weak, or unfruitful in the Vineyard of the Lord.

In this book I have made some attempt to expose the mysterious mechanisms of diverse powers, such as physical, metaphysical and spiritual powers, in the light of invisible warfare. This is to show the limitation of the powers of darkness and the limitless consciousness of the Power of the Lord, for you to experience the victory of the Lord in any area from which the wicked spirits and their human agents may rise against you.

This book is made to establish in practical terms that the limitless Power of Jesus Christ is far above and absolutely beyond the totality of all the powers of darkness. Any believer therefore who does not possess and practically demonstrate the Power of his Lord, is merely floating in the field of spiritual battle, and could become a victim.

Dear reader, let me inform .you at this point that there is no other way to possess the true Power of the Almighty God outside the perfect Blood of our Lord Jesus Christ. This is not a joke! You may be a Hindu; you may be a Buddhist; you may be a Muslim; you may even be a Pastor, Bishop, Elder, or member of a church; but without the Blood of Jesus Christ, you can never operate

Introduction

with the Highest Power of God.

Presently you may be seeking for the Power of the Almighty God through the wisdom of the entities (spirit beings) operating as "Ascended Masters", or through the Rosicrucian Order (AMORC), Grail Movement, International Society For Krishna Consciousness, Eckankar, Aetherius Society and many others. But I tell you the truth, without the recognition of the sacrifice of Blood by Our Lord Jesus Christ, the SEAL of the Highest Power, you have missed the bona-fide path of Holy POWER!

Do not be deceived. Don't allow any proclaimed MASTER, ENTITY, or SOCIETY deceive you. You may be sincerely seeking for the true Power of God. In the past I was "sincere" on the path of the occult and esoteric systems, but then I was "sincerely deceived".

Let me inform you that he who sincerely wishes to live in the practical essence of the Spirit of God, the Power of God, the Power above powers, must first of all receive JESUS CHRIST into his life. This will enable you to live in the potency of LOVE, that is His Light and Righteousness, and thus manifest His Power.

When the Spirit of Jesus comes into your life, which is Divine Love, He will cause you to uphold His holiness. Remember, HIS HOLINESS, not a man-made holiness or the holiness of a particular church. The holiness of

Behold I give unto you power

Jesus Christ is the Spirit of Power. Any "power" demonstrated outside the holiness and righteousness of Christ is bogus - it is an act of iniquity!

He who truly receives Christ into his life will in turn be received by Christ. Then the Power of God will begin to flow through him. This Power will surely flow through as many as have the Spirit of the Lord in them. To such people Christ said:

> *"Behold, I give unto you power to tread on serpents and scorpions, and over all the power of the enemy: and nothing shall by any means hurt you".*

By His Word, the Lord has already released His Power from the Highest Realm of the Godhead. His Power is very necessary in this end-time wherein all the principalities and powers of darkness are operating on the highest degree of vicious intensities.

Dear reader, never you pass over the subject matter of receiving Christ lightly, if you have not done so already. Submit fully to the Lord of Creation and let His Power come upon you!

Receive this Highest Power now!

- *Prof. Iyke Nathan Uzorma*
(Harbinger Of The Last Covenant)

CHAPTER 1

MY LETTER TO THE READER

"A wise man is strong; yea, a man of knowledge increaseth strength".

(Pro. 24:5).

Dear friend and reader of this book, **'Behold I Give Unto You Power,'** Let the Peace of the One Eternal God abide with you. Amen.

I write this letter with a sincere conviction that someone -YOU- will read it. The condition of the atmosphere is very calm in my environment as I write. Time (now) is past 6 am of Thursday 26th April, 2012. My personal prayer and meditation, which began by 3 am, ended by 4.52 am, while our spiritual family morning devotion, which began by 5.00 am, just ended at 6.11am. It is the first session of five prayer sessions today, being our prayer and fasting day.

As I sit to write this, the windows of the room are open, the air-conditioner switched off, as the fresh morning air comes in, bringing the Power, the Peace and the Blessing of the new day from the Throne of God. I received a Divine Word, a message from above, that came thus: *"say to man, what seek ye? The Power to*

Behold I give unto you power

overcome in the battles of life? Here is Power, take it; take My Power, My true Power, in the name of your Lord Jesus Christ".

THE POWER YOU SEEK

Every man needs Power, Divine Power, for victory in the journey and battles of life. Dear reader, are you in search of Power? Then here is Power, take it; read this book and understand; let it guide you on the path of blessed Power. But you must know that the Power you seek is within. Power comes from the Spirit, I mean the real Power. When your Spirit (the dormant aspects not yet activated to be expressed directly in your daily life) is quickened by the Supreme Spirit (God), you will surely become more than what you are at present. Here the Master of masters, Jesus Christ, comes in to lead and guide, for the Power you seek is within.

We must know that each man ultimately is, in a certain sense of higher reality, a manifestation of the Spirit of God in the world of gross matter. All things came into existence by the Power of God, which is the Spirit of God in motion via His Word, and are thus the manifestations of the Spirit of God at diverse levels, of which man stands on the highest level on Earth.

My letter to the reader

THE SPIRIT IS POWER

The Spirit of God is the Highest Power in all the realms of existence. The earthman is a living Soul. Every man is a Soul personality. What we know as Soul is nothing but a concentrated unit of the Spirit of God, the Breath of God, or Breath of Life.

> *"And the LORD God formed man of the dust of the ground, and breath into his nostrils the breath of life; and man became a living soul."* **(Gen. 2:7).**

The 'breath of life' which became man, a living Soul, emanates directly from God as His Spirit. This Spirit of God became concentrated into a Soul unit, an individualized unit of Divine Essence, which is the most concentrated and most potent unit of God's Spirit in the entire world of gross matter.

By the 'Universal Law of Increase' the first concentrated individualized unit of the Spirit of God on Earth (Soul) spread and became the human race. Each member of the human race, however, retains the original primordial data of the potency, propensities and paraphernalia of the first concentrated unit of God's Spirit. Reference to this Universal Law is made as follows in the Holy Scriptures;

> *"And God blessed them, and God said*

unto them, be fruitful, and multiply, and replenish the earth...."

(Gen.1:28)

"Verily, verily, I say unto you, except a corn of wheat fall into the ground and die, it abideth alone: but if it die, it bringeth forth much fruit.

(John 12: 24)

The Spirit of God is Power. The portion of THAT which became the first man is Power also. Each of the increase of THAT which was the first man is again Power. Remember, any information stored in one flash-drive can be duplicated from it into several flash-drives using the computer. And each flash-drive will retain the exact original information or material stored in the first. It follows, therefore, that each man retains and remains the initial Breath of Life or the Spirit of God in motion.

MAN: THE POWER UNIT

I have said that the Soul is a concentrated unit of the Spirit, the Spirit of God. You may understand this better when you realize that the ice-block from a refrigerator is a concentrated unit of water, that is water in another version, a concentrated individualized

My letter to the reader

version. Consequently, man is another version, a lesser version, of God. He (his Spirit) is a little version of the Supreme Spirit, the One Eternal God.

The Scripture proclaims that *"God is a Spirit"* **(Jn. 4:24)**. It also said that *"God created man in his own image."* **(Gen.1:27)**. The image of God which is man, is the version of the Spirit of God which man is. For instance, your photo image is another version of yourself in a motionless material that holds the basis by which your physical personality could be identified. Consequently, man holds the identity of God in the world of matter, space, time and energy, by virtue of the primordial Spirit which he is.

The version of the Spirit of God 'the breath of life' that is concentrated into the Soul unit, is the 'Core Essential Aspect' of man. To this end, every man via the modus-operandi of the Initial Spirit which he is, has the capacity to bring into objective and subjective manifestations the Power of the Supreme Spirit. Due to the limitation inherent in the faculties of the human gross material body, the aforementioned 'modus-operandi' and 'capacity' are very important in this connection.

Now, such modus-operandi has to be studied, via the Divine teachings of Christ, and mastered in the limited framework of the physical system of reality; in the course of which it should be understood that this 'capacity' is embedded within the mind elements. The Power flowing from the Spirit and concentrated as Soul is brought into diverse expression via the correlation of the mind faculties. There are four faculties of the mind for the purpose of normal expression of what it receives from the Soul. The entire expression of the Soul are stepped down from the mind and passed to diverse human subtle layers mental, memory, emotional including the physical aspect generally known.

The four normal faculties of the mind through which these expressions are made by the Soul are well explained in my book entitled 'The Spirit Ream'. When these faculties function in their normal order, the Power of the Spirit-Soul flows freely to the physical aspect (gross body) of man. This is maintained by divine love, inner peace and joy. But when a perversion comes into the mind system through the abnormal dichotomy of the four faculties, the fifth perverted faculty comes in, bringing it's propensities which include the five channels of vicious psychic attack. These are lust, anger, greed, vanity and attachment to mundane things.

My letter to the reader

MANIFESTING POWER

Power operates in the Physical, Metaphysical and Spiritual dimensions of existence. The pure Divine Power, the Holy Spirit, flowing to add to what the individualized Spirit (Soul) is, comes into the system of mind in which Universal Love, constant Divine Joy and Inner Peace are major channels by which an individual in Christ brings same into physical manifestation and expression.

All Powers, whether of the Holy Spirit or of the vicious occult, are correlated by the mind into objective or subjective manifestation. With the Holy Spirit, the primordial human Spirit rises in potency and comes into physical evidence via the normal faculties of the mind. When a vicious Power invades the mind and gets hold of same, through the formation of abnormal faculty, a person's life revolves directly or directly within the network of the powers of darkness, the most vicious Astral entities.

In manifesting the Power of the Spirit, however, from the Soul unit to the physical level, the Power is stepped-down at various levels from the mind to the ego, which holds the physical identity generally known. Specifically, the mind steps-down Power to the mental, memory and emotional levels; and from there to the physical level. When the awareness of Power flowing from the Spirit (the Soul unit) arrives at the physical

Behold I give unto you power

level of man, it comes into the framework of the fifteen propensities of sense data, used by the ego to stage the limitation of physical life.

The fifteen propensities of sense data include the five senses used for acquiring knowledge from the base of physical gross body. These are the ears, eyes, nose and tongue; the five working senses, which are the voice, legs, hands, anus and genital; as well as the five objects of the senses, which include smell, taste, form, touch and sound.

Power is added to man when he has the Holy Spirit, that is when the Holy Spirit encapsulates and radiates from his Soul dimension. Apart from this, all other powers demonstrated by man on the physical level, that do not rise from the Spirit which he is, begins and ends at the mind level. Vicious Powers of the occult come via the inversion of the mind by the intrusion of the most vicious Astral entities. The Power with which man can overcome the power of darkness come by the radiation of the Holy Spirit and made easy for man in the name of Jesus Christ, Lord of the Universe.

The free flow of communication from the Spirit, that is the concentrated Soul, even from the Holy Spirit, to the physical unit of man often passes through the nerves and fibers with the body. To this end, profound Noetic verdict on consciousness (the awareness unit in man) holds among other things that:

My letter to the reader

"Every nerve and fiber within the body has an unseen inner purpose. Nerve impulses travel outward from the body, along invisible pathways, in much the same manner that they travel within the body. These pathways are carriers of telepathic thoughts, impulses, and desires containing all the codified data necessary for translating any thought or image into physical actuality, altering seemingly objective events".

The fundamental teachings of Jesus Christ is the summary of the framework for the earthman to possess and manifest the Supreme Power of the Holy Spirit. The core aspects of His teachings, which enables us to demonstrate the true Power of God, can not be put into practice by anyone without the help of the Holy Spirit. But with the Holy Spirit radiating in your spirit-soul, correlated by the mind, passing through all the nerves and fibers of your body, you can live by the teachings of the Highest Lord Jesus Christ. It was to possess and physically manifest the Power of God on Earth that Christ taught man and said:

"You have heard that it was said to the people long ago, 'Do not murder, and anyone who murders will be subject to judgment'. But I tell you that anyone who is

angry with his brother will be subject to judgment. Again, anyone who says to his brother, 'Raca,' is answerable to the Sanhedrin. But anyone who says, 'You fool' will be in danger of the fire of hell.

"Therefore, if you are offering your gift at the altar and there remember that your brother has something against you, leave your gift there in front of the altar. First go and be reconciled to your brother, then come and offer your gift. Settle matters quickly with your adversary who is taking you to court. Do it while you are still with him on the way or he may hand you over to the judge, and the judge may hand you over to the officer, and you may be thrown into prison.

"You have heard that it was said, 'Eye for eye, and Tooth for tooth'. But I tell you, Do not Resist an evil person. If someone strikes you on the right cheek, turn to him the other also. And if someone wants to sue you and take your tunic, let him have your cloak as well. If someone forces you to go one mile, go with him two miles. Give to the one who wants to borrow from you.

"You have heard that it was said, 'Love

My letter to the reader

your neighbor and hate your enemy', But I tell you: Love your enemies and pray for those who persecute you, that you may be Sons of your Father in heaven. He causes his sun to rise on the evil and the good, and sends rain on the righteous and the unrighteous". (Math. 5:21-25,38-45; New International Version)

POWER BEYOND THE SURFACE

Every man, the man in Christ, the man who practically upholds the teachings of Our Lord Jesus Christ, can bring into manifestation the Power of the Holy Spirit. Now, within the essence of the Spirit which is man, every man is the same in the journey of life, but all men are not on the same level. From the dimension of the Spirit, what one man is, another man is. The difference is on three basic factors.

First, the degree of what you know about Power determines what you can do with Power in practical terms. Thus, the knowledge of this is very important. Your knowledge in this regard, even in human's terms, is a point of difference between you and those bereft of such knowledge. The second factor of difference comes when the mind is invaded and ruled by the vicious occult powers. A person at this point will make a difference in the midst of others, from the system of vicious crafts and manipulations of darkness.

The third and highest factor of difference from one man to another is the Eternal Spirit Divine, The Holy Spirit. When the Holy Spirit gets hold, comes in, or begins to radiate in your concentrated Soul unit, you become in human terms what may be called extraordinary spiritual person. The Holy Spirit puts you in constant daily consciousness of the Almighty God and gives you the inner ability to practice Universal Love as taught by the Greatest Lord Jesus Christ.

Some humans have demonstrated powers from all the three factors; some from two factors; while some from a single factor. Nevertheless, all the factors of difference from man to man, serve as evidence of the fact that there are powers operating beyond the mere surface of physical life. As you may know, hidden powers have come forth and practically demonstrated through diverse human channels. Throughout the life of man in all ages, there have been manifestations of Power and powers arising from different factors, to show in practical terms that there are more than the eyes can see. Thus, it became evident that there are powers that lie beyond the physical aspects generally known to humans.

Now, on a personal note: My experience within the

My letter to the reader

framework of the foregoing factors, is certainly my foremost evidence in this regard. Thus, I speak from what I know in practical terms. Furthermore, regarding the demonstration of Power and powers, we read in the Holy Scriptures and in some writings of antiquity, read in our time, amongst others, that:

The Great Prophet Moses of ancient Israel, divided the red sea for the children of Israel to pass through, amongst others.

The rods of the 'wise men' of Egypt changed to serpents that were swallowed by that of Moses.

Shri Krishna of the Yadu dynasty, Mathura, ancient India, caused stones to float on the water, using same to build a palace upon the sea, amongst others.

The shadow of Saint Peter, leader of the Apostles of Jesus Christ, healed several sick people, amongst others.

Kammeje of Isuochi, South East Nigeria, changed into hundreds of butterflies that arose to the sky and disappeared, to mark the end of life on Earth, amongst others.

The Jewish Prophet Daniel, while in the land of Persia, was unharmed in the midst of hungry lions, amongst others.

Behold I give unto you power

The foot of Shri Anandamurti of present India, founder of 'Ananda Marga Yoga Society, had high electric current that electrocute people to death, amongst others.

Paul Twetchell of the United States of America, Living Eck Master and founder of Eckankar, ran upon the sea, amongst others.

Samson, the Great Warrior of ancient Israel, had Power on his hair to bamboozle and defeat his enemies.

Rabazar Tarzs, the great Lama of Tibet, has lived for over five hundred years physically in the Himalaya Mountains, and others like him, amongst others.

Obribon Okpo of Oron, South South, Nigeria, lived above his people of the time. After his death and during his burial, thousands of strange birds came from the sky, took his corpse away back into the sky, amongst others.

King David of ancient Israel, as a boy, used mere stones to defeat and destroy the great giant Goliath in the field of battle, amongst others.

Muhammed al-Muntaza of Shiraz, who did not marry and never had a child, disappeared without

My letter to the reader

death at the cave of the Mosque
which he was proclaimed the 'M
One) and 'Muntaza' (Expected
others.

- Hiranyakashipu, the most powe
ever lived, and the most viciou
India, for the purpose of accumu
powers, stood on one foot at a s
years, amongst others.

- The Great Prophet of Israel,
chariots of fire into the sky, amo

- Siddhartha Gautama (Buddha)
fought and defeated a mighty ev
forest, amongst others.

- Sir George King of England,
Aetherius Society' and 'Primary
Channel', communicated with
Beings in other Planets and rece
on Earth, amongst others.

- Sanjaya, the 'wise man of an
Confidential Secretary of th
Dhrtarastra, while in the palace
away from the battle field of Ku
accurate vision and gave perfec
king of the battle situation, amo

39

Behold I give unto you power

Balaam the son of Beor, Prophet of ancient Moab, saw accurate visions with his eyes opened, amongst others.

Nostradamus of France and Mother Shipton of Scotland, in their times saw the future of the human race as presently constituted, amongst others.

Shadrach, Meshach and Abednego, the three Jewish faithfuls, were completely unharmed in the great fire of Nebuchanezzar while in Babylon.

Caitanya Mahaprabhu of Bengal, who introduced the Vaishnava Maha Mantra, disappeared into the deity of Jaganath while dancing spiritual songs in Puri, amongst others.

Trinita of Goma, Democratic Republic of Congo, spoke the day he was born in February, 1990, amongst others.

OUR LORD JESUS CHRIST

These and a host of others in different parts of the world, at diverse times, show quite clearly that there are powers operating far beyond the surface of man's physical life. Nevertheless, when we

My letter to the reader

talk of Power, Our Lord Jesus Christ stands at the peak of it all. He proves that He does not only demonstrate the highest Power, but that He is the consummate manifestation of the Highest Power Himself. He is Himself the Highest Power in the Universe. All Powers in all the realms of life are completely under His control. To this end, He declared: *"...All Power is given unto me in heaven and in earth"*.

Furthermore, He is the One and the only Man who informed people of how He would die and resurrect from the grave and went ahead to do so. The death and resurrection of The Son of Man, Jesus Christ of Nazareth, Israel, is the Highest Power ever demonstrated in the world of man. Thus, through His teachings, life, works, death and resurrection, Our Lord Jesus Christ displayed the Highest and True Power of the Almighty God, for all the generations of men. He also said:

> *"Fear not; I am the first and the last: I am He that liveth, and was dead; and behold, I am alive for evermore, Amen; and have the keys of hell and of death"*. **(Rev. 1:17,18)**.

Anyone who seeks for Power to enable him overcome the vicious powers in the field of the battles of life, will find it in Christ Jesus if he is sincere enough. Christ is the Power. Therefore, being POWER Himself, He is in the best position to give us the Power of victory, as He said:

Behold I give unto you power

"BEHOLD, I GIVE UNTO YOU POWER TO TREAD ON SERPENTS AND SCORPIONS, AND OVER ALL THE POWER OF THE ENEMY: AND NOTHING SHALL BY ANY MEANS HURT YOU." **(Luke 10:19).**

At this point, dear reader, it is important to understand that the existence of Jesus Christ is not a joke; it is not a mere religious affair, it is not a matter limited to the organized churches of our time; neither is it a matter of merely attending a church. This is a matter of the legitimate POWER of God in eternity. This Power seeks to be possessed and demonstrated in the world of man by any human who has Christ, the True Spirit of Christ Jesus, in himself and is worthy to express Divine Love, which Christ is.

Receive this Power NOW!

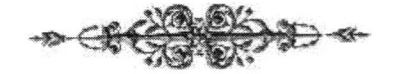

CHAPTER 2

DIVERSE POWERS

"But when the multitudes saw it, they marveled and glorified God, which had given such power unto men"
(Math. 9:8).

I bear witness that the Power of God is real; for daily in my inner understanding I do practically experience this pure Spiritual Power beyond all that words can express. This is the experience which Christ has provided for every believer.

The Supreme Power of the Almighty God is here now. This Power seeks to pass through you to do the work of the Lord, only if you submit fully to Him. You may be willing to submit to the Power of the Godhead and manifest the same Power in the world of man, but at the same time you may be hindered in this regard by either your mental or emotional propensities. His Power, however, is already given to every child of God: take it or leave it, according to the relationship of your inner-man with the Spirit of Christ.

Now, when Christ said: *"Behold, I give unto you power"*, what kind of Power did He give? First of all, it is important to understand that there are three major aspects or kinds of power in the Universe. These correspond with the major systems of reality of all the realms of existence. They also correspond with the tripartite nature of the earthman.

THREE MAJOR ASPECTS OF POWER

It is said in the Scripture that man has *"body, soul and spirit: "...and I pray God your whole spirit and soul and body be preserved blameless unto the coming of our Lord Jesus Christ"* **(1 Thess. 5:23).** These are the three major aspects of man - Body, Soul and Spirit. And there are three major aspects of power that man can possess and manifest, according to his three major aspects of existence. These include the:

PHYSICAL POWER
METAPHYSICAL POWER
SPIRITUAL POWER

The body of the earthman operates in the realms of the gross material power (physical power) within the physical system of reality. The human Soul operates in the realms of subtle power within the mind's metaphysical system of reality. The Soul, to this end, encapsulates the mind, the dream-body and other related subtle bodies. While the human Spirit operates in the essence of multidimensional Power within the spiritual system of reality.

RECOGNITION OF YOUR LEVEL OF POWER

I will soon analyze the three major aspects of powers, so that you may recognize the Power with which the believer could tread on "serpents and scorpions", as set forth by Our Lord Jesus Christ. But we have to understand that all these powers are available for man here and now.

This exposition will also enable you comprehend the level of your power, that is the particular aspect of power under which you are now operating. Let no one deceive himself and claim to be what he is not. Therefore if you discover in reality, via this treatise, that you are below on the strata of the true Power of the Lord, the Power which He gave, you can still rise in the strength of His Spirit and come to the path of the Highest Power.

Simply stated: physical power is very much below metaphysical power in all aspects of operation. To this end, one on a higher dimension of metaphysical power can completely dominate or control one operating solely on the level of the physical system of power.

Furthermore, the metaphysical power is far below and absolutely minute as far as Spiritual Power is concerned. The Spiritual Power is the true Power of the Lord. This is the only Power that is endless in eternity. One with this Power has what is far above all powers. It is with this Power that we can completely overcome all the powers of darkness in the field of spiritual warfare.

You may think that you have the true Power of the Lord. But be informed that your thinking is not enough in this connection. Do you truly possess the pure Spiritual Power of the Lord God Almighty? I mean do you possess this Power in practical demonstration? You may find out as we continue.

PHYSICAL POWER

The physical power has many units of itself available for man within his physical system of existence. But let it be emphasized that no earthman can overcome the powers of darkness (serpents and scorpions) even with the multitude of physical powers found in the world of man.

This is so because the subtle powers used by the Prince of Darkness and his proclaimed wicked spirits against the children of men, operate on a level far

Diverse powers

beyond the totality of all the powers operating solely within the physical system of reality. But in the physical system, however, the earthman can uphold, manipulate, or manifest certain units of power inherent in the physical world of gross matter. Now let us consider few of the several units of physical power in the world of man.

STRENGTH: The human strength is a unit of power within the physical system of existence. Now, all men are not on the same degree of strength. You may manifest higher or lesser degree of strength, because it is given to the earthman to manifest diverse degrees of physical strength. Nevertheless, no amount of physical strength in you can overcome the powers of darkness. Thus, this is not the power which the Lord gave us in this connection, when He said, "Behold, I give unto you power"

The Scripture says: *"It is not by strength that one prevails".* **(See I Sam. 2:9, New International Version).** If you rely on your human strength in the field of spiritual warfare, you will surely be defeated, because a little witchcraft can knock you off - then you are gone! Again it is written: *"...not by might, nor by power, but by my Spirit, saith the Lord of hosts"* **(Zach. 4:6)**

MATERIAL WEALTH: Material wealth (money) is another unit of power within the physical system of reality. One who has riches in earthly terms, could possess and manifest great opulence of material power. But it is evident that no amount of financial power can deliver an earthman from the manipulations of the Prince of Darkness. I am saying this categorically because I was highly involved in a vicious occult network and esoteric manipulations.

It is true that with financial power, or material wealth, you can do many things in the physical world. Yes, with material wealth you may even reach the highest degree of temporal enjoyment and gratification of the material senses. There is no doubt about this.

Nevertheless, if you are outside the perfect righteousness of our Lord Jesus Christ, then regardless of your earthly wealth, you are totally invalid in the light of the invisible warfare going on in this world. Often some people think that when one has great riches and material wealth, it means he is "rich in heaven". This is a wrong thinking in the light of the Scriptures. The truth is that if you have material wealth without the Holy Spirit at the centre of your life, then you are spiritually poor and blind. Listen to the Words of the Lord:

> *"Because you say: I am rich and have acquired riches and do not need anything at all, but you do not know you are miserable and pitiable and poor and blind and naked. I advise you to buy from me gold refined by fire that you may become rich, and white outer*

garments that you may become dressed and that the shame of your nakedness may not become manifested, and eyesalve to rub in your eyes that you may see". (Rev. 3:17,18, New World Translation of the Holy Scriptures).

POLITICAL AUTHORITY: Political authority is also a major unit of power exercised by the earthman in the physical system of reality. To this end, a President or Prime Minister of a country has higher degrees of political power among his people. But can any amount of political power exercised by a President, a Prime Minister or even by a military Head of State, overcome the games of the Prince of Darkness? Surely this is not the Power with which we could overcome the forces of darkness. For no amount of political power can deliver the earthman from the manipulations of "serpents and scorpions".

JUDICIAL AUTHORITY: What about judicial authority? A judge, for instance, has the judicial power to imprison his fellow man or even condemn him to death. But a judge can not command an evil spirit to flee on the strength of his judicial power. For the powers of darkness to flee from you, you need something more than judicial power.

ELECTRICAL POWER: This is one of the greatest units of power found in the physical system of reality.

Behold I give unto you power

The earthman has done several things in this world via the use of electrical power. And sincerely speaking, the influence of this power is overwhelming. Nevertheless, the children of men can not tread on serpents and scorpions, as spoken by Christ, on the strength of electrical power.

NUCLEAR POWER: Again, I am sure you are aware of the potency of nuclear energy. It is said that, in terms of destruction, this is the highest power found in the physical system of reality. Nevertheless, it is absolutely evident that no amount of nuclear power can enable the earthman destroy the invisible powers of darkness.

Now, there are still other units of power found in the world of man. But each and every power exercised by the earthman in the physical system of reality, are invalid in the light of the Power set forth by Christ, with which the believer can tread on all the powers of darkness. The Power spoken of by Christ is THE SUPREME POWER. With this Power, the believer is on top of all the powers in the Universe. With this Power also, you can decree and decide what happens in all realms of physical and metaphysical powers.

METAPHYSICAL POWER

The metaphysical power is a subtle power that lies beyond the realm of all the units of physical power. Within the three systems of power - PHYSICAL, METAPHYSICAL and SPIRITUAL - the metaphysical power is the immediate power beyond the physical system of reality.

Some people who are established within the metaphysical system of power, are wrongly of the thought that they are great champions in the realm of Spiritual Power. But in reality they are far below the realm of Spiritual Power.

There are even some members and officials of the church who are also involved in this wrong thinking. To some people, however, any power beyond the physical system of existence is "spiritual power", but this is not true, because there are different units of power found within the metaphysical dimension, yet they are all far below the true realm of Spiritual Power. And all the metaphysical units of power are summarized in five headings. In other words, there are five major kinds of power within the subtle or metaphysical system of reality. They include:

MENTAL POWER
EMOTIONAL POWER

PSYCHIC POWER
OCCULT POWER
ESOTERIC POWER

Now, let me briefly speak on the five metaphysical units of power, to guide us towards the recognition of the reality of the level of power wherein each of us is presently established. I want us to examine these units of power for each reader to know whether he is operating within or beyond the realm of metaphysical consciousness.

MENTAL POWER: The mental power is the lowest unit of power within the metaphysical system of reality. The mental power includes the use of higher retentive memory, the ability to remember and think fast, the ability of profound mental speculation, as well as the use of higher logical analysis, to mention but a few. Within this framework lies the ability to remember, quote or recite verses of the Scripture, but without true Divine Power. Diverse mundane philosophies also come from this system.

One may be highly advanced in the realm of mental power, but no one can tread on "serpents and scorpions" even with the highest degree of mental power. This is so because "serpents and scorpions" (powers of darkness) have their realm of existence beyond the mental level of recognition.

Diverse powers

There are some of us today who are highly advanced in the realm of mental power, but are still bereft of the true Power spoken of by Our Lord Jesus Christ. For instance, some of us on the mental level may use the mental power to memorize several chapters and verses of the Holy Scriptures, and often use same in our preaching and prayers. This is good! But if you don't have the Spirit of Christ in you, (the Spirit of the Holiness and Righteousness of the Lord God Almighty), then you can never overcome the Prince of Darkness even with several Scriptural verses on your head.

For further example: a church 'pastor' operating solely within this limited realm of mental consciousness, may preach and profoundly analyze the workings of the Great Power of the Almighty God which manifested through Moses, Daniel, Paul and many others, yet the same 'pastor' can not manifest this Power because he is on a lower strata of power, mental power.

Consequently, there are many proclaimed 'men of God' who can preach and teach others about the limitless Power of the Almighty God, but who, nevertheless, can do little or nothing as far as the practical aspect of manifesting and demonstrating this very Power is concerned. The preaching of the Gospel on the mental level can not bring healing, true salvation, deliverance, spiritual victory and righteousness. But the preaching of the Gospel on the platform of Spiritual Power brings these and much more.

Behold I give unto you power

> *"And Jesus went about all the cities and villages, teaching in their synagogues, and preaching the gospel of the kingdom, and healing every sickness and every disease among the people"* **(Matt. 9:35)**.

When you speak to the children of men about the Kingdom of Heaven on the platform of Power, as demonstrated by Jesus Christ, every sickness and disease must be wiped off. But if you do so on the platform of your mental power, nothing will happen in this connection. Our Lord Jesus Christ preached on the platform of the Highest Power, which is Himself, thus He was able to heal every sickness and every disease among the people. This is what we are expected to do when we are strengthened by His Spirit.

Furthermore, a believer who lives in the limited essence of mental power, requires or follows a systematic process in all matters of transcendental reality and spiritual existence. This process, however, is misleading. This is because spiritual or transcendental reality is multidimensional and not systematic. The systematic approach therefore is the outcome of mental recognition.

To this end, you may be a Bishop, Pastor, Archbishop, Pope, Deacon, Evangelist, Elder, or Apostle, but if you are on the mental level, you are not better than the High

Diverse powers

Priest who lived during the earthly mission of Our Lord Jesus Christ: and surely you will fail in the field of spiritual warfare. There is no way you can overcome the powers of darkness if you are on the mental level of power.

EMOTIONAL POWER: The second unit of power within the metaphysical system of reality, is the emotional power. It is said that the Kingdom of God is not a matter of much talking, but of practical demonstration of Power. However, 'believers' on the emotional level also belong to the group of much talking without Power. Though the emotional level is higher than the mental level, yet the emotional power, no matter how great, can not tread on "serpents and scorpions".

Now, a believer operating on the level of the emotional propensity of metaphysical power is like a big gun that makes much noise but has no single bullet. The gun can make noise but can not kill even a fly, because it has no bullet. The bullet in this connection is the Power of God that is mighty through Christ for pulling down the strongholds of the Prince of Darkness. The BULLET is the POWER that KILLS the ENEMY. Without this 'bullet', you may make great noise, but you can not prevail in the field of spiritual battle. Are you a big gun without bullet? Do you make great noise without God's Power? Think about this!

Furthermore, it is important to note that the influence

Behold I give unto you power

of emotional power on a believer, during his personal worship of God or while he worships in the midst of the congregation of the children of God, may lead him to sweet talks and illusory phantasmagoria. These he may further consider in his wrong thinking to be the 'Great Power of the Almighty God'. Again he may even manipulate his voice during this period and 'speak in tongues', via the influence of this emotional propensity. But when this is done, he still submits to the wrong thinking that the Holy Ghost has come down, or has come upon him.

Nevertheless, the difference is very clear. The Holy Ghost Power is Absolute and for ever beyond the little emotional unit of the human consciousness. The Holy Ghost is the consummate Supreme Potency of the Godhead which is Omnipresent. But the emotional power operates via a faculty of the mind of the earthman.

When the Holy Ghost comes down to operate through you or upon you, there are diverse and specific manifestations of the Glorious Power of the Living God Jehovah via the mighty name of the Lord - JESUS CHRIST. The Holy Ghost brings solution to every human problem. But when the emotional power is in control, surely great noise will be made but you will return home without practical solution - empty!

It is true, however, that some believers 'speak in tongues' under the influence of emotional power, while

Diverse powers

some do so under the influence of the Holy Ghost. Those who do this via the emotional propensity should know it. This is because they are consciously involved in manipulating their tongues in this regard. But those who are overwhelmed by the Holy Ghost to speak in tongues, are not involved in this conscious manipulation of tongue.

Now, those highly established in the realm of emotional power, may even 'cry' during the period of their personal or congregational worship of the Lord; they may even 'repent' of their sins in the mode of crying via the emotional propensity. But when the emotional power expires after few hours, days, weeks or months, they return back to their sin. This is because the power that impelled them to 'cry' and 'repent' is the limited emotional power and not the limitless Power of Christ.

Sincerely speaking, many people who claim to be true believers today, operate under the level of emotional power of the mind. Again there is no way one can overcome principalities and powers of darkness via the use of emotional power; for the Prince of Darkness and his empire of wicked spirits operate beyond the realm of emotional consciousness within the metaphysical system of reality.

PSYCHIC POWER: The psychic power is the third unit of power within the metaphysical system of existence. The psychic power is higher and stronger than both the mental and the emotional units of metaphysical power. This power manifests in diverse forms. The psychic power can manifest in man and other creatures via a natural process set up by the Creator God. This very power can also be corrupted to manifest in man and other creatures via a process initiated by the manipulations of the powers of darkness.

To this end, within the hierarchy of the powers of darkness, there are principalities and powers of darkness ('serpents and scorpions') operating as 'psychic entities'. The vicious psychic entities therefore are the spirits advancing the use of psychic power for the promotion of the crafts and devices of the kingdoms of darkness.

The truth remains, however, that psychic power can be used either for good or evil. It can be used for good through the natural or the normal process set up by God. It can also be used for evil through the abnormal process caused by the manipulation of the forces of darkness.

For instance, intuition is a natural psychic power planted in the human consciousness by God, to enable us know or realize certain things without thinking it out. May be someone is coming to see you without you knowing of it, but before he knocks at your door, you had a sudden realization that someone is coming to see you. That is intuition. It is a natural psychic power which the Creator God planted in man for good. When one is pure in Christ, his intuitive faculty works solely to the glory

Diverse powers

of God. But if one is an agent of darkness, his intuitive faculty works to promote the crafts of the wicked spirits.

For further example: some roots and herbs contain substance of psychic power which, when refined become drugs, such as tablets and injections used to cure or prevent an ailment This substance of psychic power, however, is naturally planted in such roots and herbs by the Creator God. There is also a natural psychic power planted by God on water, sand, oil, waves, winds, lightning's stroke, sun-rays, the human eye and thunder, to mention but a few, which operate for good, but may also operate for evil when contaminated by the powers of darkness.

Now, the art of physiognomy, palmistry, shadow-reading graphology and geomancy, are some of the units of subtle framework of transcendental powers via the psychic unit of power. The aforementioned psychic units are often worked out via the Astral powers. However, the Spirit of God can also awaken these in a certain dimension of true Divine Knowledge, but in specific personal and not in general terms.

I have earlier stated that psychic power is greater than both the mental and the emotional units of metaphysical power. To this end, an agent of darkness with enormous psychic power can bring harm to a 'churchman' on the mental and the emotional levels. It was even reported awhile ago how thunder killed a certain 'churchman' inside a church in Warri, Nigeria. That 'churchman' surely was bereft of the Power required via the Blood of Christ. He was merely a member of a church, and not a member of the movement of the limitless Power of Jehovah God operating via Christ, hence he was killed by agents of darkness, who utilized the psychic force of thunder via the manipulations of the Prince of Darkness.

OCCULT POWER: The occult power is the next unit of power beyond the psychic level within the realm of metaphysical power. The vicious occult power in totality, however, is purely a negative power - the power of darkness. One can naturally manifest some degrees of mental, emotional and psychic powers without being an agent of darkness. But one can not possess or manifest any degree of the dark occult power without being an agent of darkness.

When Our Lord Jesus Christ spoke of "serpents and scorpions", He was speaking of all the powers of darkness mostly concentrated for evil within the occult unit of metaphysical power. In the past, I used psychic, occult and esoteric powers in diverse ways. (see the book: OCCULT GRAND MASTER NOW IN CHRIST, by Iyke Nathan Uzorma).

In the past also I possessed and utilized greater degrees of occult power in the circle of Grandmasters. Even at the age of fifteen, I used this power to completely influence and control others, see physically

Diverse powers

without my eyes, vanish into the air when necessary, read sealed letters, bend strong iron via the projection of my eyes, project (transfer) myself and live briefly inside another human being, animal, tree (etc), render gun or knife ineffective when applied on me, among other feats.

Now, witches and wizards, operating within the highest hierarchy of any of the four major units of witchcraft spirits (Black, White, Kali, Abra Melin), are custodians of higher occult power. In the past also I was a Master of the hierarchy of the witches of Abra Melin operating at Gobi desert near Afghanistan. (see the book: HOW TO COMPLETELY OVERCOME WITCHES AND WIZARDS AND ALL THE POWERS OF DARKNESS, by lyke Nathan Uzorma).

Please be warned: **If you are a 'believer' on the mental level, or you are a 'believer' highly involved in the realm of emotional power; without the endless Power of the Lord, you can not overcome occult power in the field of battle. You can not run beyond your shadow. You can not use what you don't have.**

To this end, you need something higher than the occult power and all the units of metaphysical power. And not just a higher power, but the POWER which is the HIGHEST. Yes, the Highest Power is here now. I am speaking of the true Power, of Jesus Christ. You need the Power in the Blood of Christ. Surely this is the Supreme Power!

Behold I give unto you power

ESOTERIC POWER: The esoteric power is the last and the highest unit of metaphysical power. This is the most concentrated power within the hierarchy of all the astro-metaphysical systems. The esoteric power is greater than the occult power. This is the invisible power directly exercised by the Prince of Darkness, the mighty satanic spirit beings of the realms beyond, controlling deities (Prince) of nations, satanic arch spirits, vicious spirits in the order of ascended masters, higher disembodied entities of the realm of darkness and vicious space masters, to mention but a few.

Furthermore, the vicious esoteric power is the very power used by all the principal human agents of the powers of darkness operating on Earth as grandmasters. The darkest grandmasters are human beings empowered by darkness to lead the game of falsehood and manipulations. In the past I served at this level via the command of the hierarchy of the powers of darkness.

In this world of man, the esoteric power appears to be very great and highly potent invisible power. Consequently, the esoteric vicious adepts and grandmasters use this power to manipulate the children of men and lead them astray via diverse channels and means. The esoteric power is the principal power that co-ordinates all the units of metaphysical power for the promotion of the crafts and devices of satanic kingdom.

It is true also that esoteric power of the metaphysical

Diverse powers

system of the Prince of Darkness can duplicate some of the things done via the Supreme Power of the true Lord of the Universe. But the esoteric power has a limit to which it can go in this regard. Nevertheless, the Power of the Godhead is unlimited in eternity.

As such, in the light of the Supreme Power of the Sole Ultimate Reality, as revealed to us via Our Lord Jesus Christ, the esoteric power is completely inconsequential. To the earthman, the esoteric power is great. But in the Presence of Jesus Christ, the esoteric power can not exist - it must disappear and fade away. All powers in the universe are forever below Christ, for it is written:

> *"For by Him (CHRIST) were all things created, that are in heaven, and that are in earth, visible and invisible, whether they be thrones, or dominions, or principalities, or powers; all things were created by Him, and for Him"* **(Col. 1:16)**.

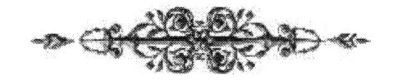

CHAPTER 3

THE HIGHEST POWER

"Which by His strength setteth fast the mountains; being girded with power"
(Psm. 65:6)

Spiritual Power is the Highest Power. The Spiritual Power is surely the Power above powers. This is the Highest Power. It is the last Power. This is the Sole Ultimate Power proceeding directly out of the Throne of the Godhead. This is the Power which Christ gave us when He said:

"Behold, I give unto you power to tread on serpents and scorpions, and over all the power of the enemy: and nothing shall by any means hurt you".

When the Spiritual Power of the Lord God Almighty is upon you, you are far above the vicious powers and nothing in the Universe will hurt you. Again, when this Almighty Power is in operation, everything must bow. The Prince of Darkness, with his principalities and powers, must flee from the rays of the Light of this Power which is Christ.

The highest power

Now, the Angels of God, the Arch-angels, the Living Creatures, the Ancient Ones (Elders) and all the might, invisible beings operating in the essence of the Holy Spirit, have diverse levels within the multidimensional Power of the spiritual system of the Almighty God. The children of God on Earth also have diverse degrees or levels of anointing within this realm of God's Power.

Nevertheless, no matter your degree of anointing of the Power of God, whether great or small, all the powers of darkness must bow to you. The smallest anointing of the Power of God is greater than the greatest power of the realm of darkness. Therefore when one who proclaims Christ is afraid of witches, poison, demons and other elements of darkness, such a person truly does not believe in the limitless Power of Our Lord Jesus Christ, and he has not experienced the Supreme Power that I am talking of. The Power of God is Omnipresent, and by this Power the entire creation is daily sustained. A true child of God is a channel through which the Power of God operates.

> *"And these signs shall follow them that believe; In my name shall they cast out devils; they shall speak with new tongues; they shall take up serpents; and if they drink any deadly thing, it shall not hurt them; they shall lay hands on the sick, and they shall recover"* **(Mark 16:17,18)**

Behold I give unto you power

ESOTERIC VERSUS SPIRITUAL

When you study the Holy Scriptures, you will discover the constant conflict of spiritual and metaphysical powers. You will further discover that Spiritual Power (THE POWER OF GOD) has always prevailed in each and every conflict. For instance, in the days of Moses, the great servant of God, the superiority of Spiritual Power over all the metaphysical powers of Egypt was evident and irresistible.

The Power of the Living God Jehovah was demonstrated in Egypt through Moses at a time when a great Master of esoteric power also lived in Egypt. This Master, known as and called 'Gopal Das', was reported to be the "Mahanta" of his time. (Mahanta means "Godman" or "the manifestation of God"). His name (Gopal Das) is of the Sanskrit India whilst he lived in Egypt.

It is said that Gopal Das lived on Earth for more than five hundred years. He did not marry neither did he begot children. As a matter of fact, he was reported to be a great 'Spirit Being' that took a human form and lived in the world of man, and he lived without an earthly father and mother.

Now Gopal Das is recognized in the Ancient Order of Vairagi of the Himalaya Mountains of India as one of

The highest power

their Ascended Masters. It was this Ancient Order of Vairagi that brought the Eckankar Society to the general public, through Paul Twitchell of USA, who was spiritually trained by the mighty Spirit Beings operating as The Nine Silent Ones under the guide of Rabazar Tarzs. This Rabazar Tarzs, who is presently on Earth, has also lived for more than five hundred years both at the Himalaya Mountains and Agam-Des of Tibet.

Presently Gopal Das is in the Astral realm - the first occult kingdom of the air. There he is incharge of a mystery school, or esoteric training centre, known as 'The Temple of Golden Wisdom'. This secret temple of the metaphysical system houses the 'Fourth Section of the Shariyat-ki-Sugmad'. Higher students of esoteric mysteries on Earth do go for studies in this mystery school especially in the night, via astral projection or soul travel.

In the land of ancient Egypt, Gopal Das was the "Hidden Godman" worshipped by all the Pharaohs of his time. Through him different crafts of the esoteric consciousness flourished and prevailed among the Egyptians. The Masters of Vairagi of India and Tibet, the students and Masters of Eckankar world-wide and some of the higher initiates of esoteric mysteries, knew that Moses lived on Earth at the time when Pharaoh was the foremost secret disciple of Gopal Das, who then lived in a cave.

Behold I give unto you power

This being (Gopal Das) also trained several adepts and masters of psychic, occult and esoteric mysteries who served the king of Egypt (Pharaoh) as "wise men". Among these wise men include highly advanced magicians, sorcerers, astrologers, necromancers, wizards etc. To this end, Gopal Das was the "god" of Pharaoh. He was the manifestation of the highest esoteric power. But what happened when the metaphysical powers of Gopal Das and all the powers of Egypt met with the Supreme Power of the God of Moses Jehovah?

When the Lord God Almighty called Moses, He also told him: "See, I have made thee a god to Pharaoh; and Aaron thy brother shall be thy prophet" (Exo. 7:1). Pharaoh was already used to the concept and worship of "man as God". Gopal Das was a god made for Pharaoh and all the Egyptians by the hierarchy of the highest esoteric power. And the Living God also set forth Moses as a god to Pharaoh. This brought one of the greatest conflicts of spiritual and metaphysical powers, to show the Power above powers.

At first when Moses spoke to Pharaoh in the name of the Living Almighty Jehovah, Pharaoh derided the true Lord because he thought that no power in the universe is beyond the esoteric power of the Egyptian avatars, adepts and grandmasters. Pharaoh categorically told Moses at the initial stage: "...Who is Jehovah, so that I should obey his voice to send Israel away? I do not know

Jehovah at all..." (Exo. 5:2, New World Translation of the Holy Scriptures).

ENCOUNTER OF POWERS

As Moses stood before Pharaoh, he used the Highest Spiritual Power to perform miracles. But the occult and esoteric grandmasters (wise men) of Egypt also duplicated some of the miracles of Moses via their highly concentrated esoteric powers. Then Pharaoh and the people were bamboozled: which one is the true power? Who holds the Highest Power above powers? Some people may have wanted to know. Moses and his "prophet" Aaron were there. The magicians were there also. The king of Egypt was watching. The Jews then may have wanted to witness the Power of the very God who had sent Moses. The Scripture says:

> *"And Moses and Aaron went in unto Pharaoh, and they did so as the LORD had commanded: and Aaron cast down his rod before Pharaoh, and before his servants, and it became a serpent. Then Pharaoh also called the wise men and the sorcerers: now the magicians of Egypt, they also did in like manner with their*

enchantments. For they cast down every man his rod, and they became serpents: but Aaron's rod swallowed up their rods" (Exo. 7:10-12).

Here was a practical demonstration of spiritual and esoteric powers, to decide which is which; to prove the Power above powers. On one side was Moses and Aaron operating with the Supreme Spiritual Power of the Living God whilst on the other side were the wizards, sorcerers, grandmasters and magicians of Egypt with the highest powers of the occult and esoteric systems. The rod of Moses, which he gave to Aaron, changed and became a strong serpent in the presence of the king of Egypt. This was done by the limitless Power of the true Lord: the Highest Spiritual Power of God was in motion and the rod became a serpent.

Then the magicians came. They were not charlatans or imbeciles in the art of the manipulation of psychic, occult and esoteric powers. Rather they were bona-fide masters and grandmasters in this regard. Consequently, and by virtue of the multitude of their powers, the rods of the magicians and sorcerers also changed and became serpents. It was now one serpent versus many serpents. Pharaoh was watching. He knew that the strong must overcome the weak. At this point the superiority of the Living Power of God prevailed; for the rod of Moses became the supreme serpent of serpents. Then the rod of Moses swallowed up all the rod of the wise men of Egypt.

The highest power
DUPLICATION OF SPIRITUAL POWER

The changing of rods into serpents via spiritual and metaphysical powers was not the end, as the practical demonstration of powers continued. **Exodus chapter 7 verses 20 and 22** added:

> *"And Moses and Aaron did so as the LORD commanded; and he lifted up the rod, and smote the waters that were in the river, in the sight of Pharaoh, and in the sight of his servants; and all the waters in the river turned to blood... And the magicians of Egypt did so with their enchantments...."*

When this happened, (that is when Moses and the magicians turned water to blood), Pharaoh and those with him may have wrongly thought that Moses and the wise men of Egypt were operating on the same system of power. With their material senses, they could not comprehend that Moses and Aaron were operating on the infinite essence of the Power of the true God within the spiritual system, far above all the metaphysical powers of the proclaimed masters, grandmasters, wizards and avatars of Egypt. This wrong thinking was the more revived in them after the experience in **Exodus chapter 8 verses 5 to 7**. There we read:

> *"And the Lord spake unto Moses, say unto*

Behold I give unto you power

> *Aaron, stretch forth thine hand with thy rod over the streams, over the rivers, and over the ponds, and cause frogs to come up upon the land of Egypt; and the frogs came up, and covered the land of Egypt. And the magicians did so with their enchantments, and brought up frogs upon the land of Egypt".*

This was yet another evidence of the duplication of the Power of God by the agents of darkness. But this duplication has a limit to which it can go. The Power of God is unlimited, whereas the powers of the psychic, occult and esoteric systems are minute and for ever limited.

However, Pharaoh and his people saw that frogs manifested from the realms beyond by virtue of the invisible powers exercised by Moses and the Egyptian magicians. This was enough for them to conclude that the occult grandmasters, esoteric avatars, necromancers, sorcerers, wizards and magicians of Egypt will surely duplicate each and every miracle performed by Moses and Aaron. But what happened next? Listen:

> *"And the LORD said unto Moses, say unto Aaron, stretch out thy rod, and smite the dust of the land, that it may become lice throughout all the land of Egypt. And they*

did so; for Aaron stretched out his hand with his rod, and smote the dust of the earth, and it became lice in man, and in beast; all the dust of the land became lice throughout all the land of Egypt. And the magicians did so with their enchantments to bring forth lice, but they could not: so there were lice upon man, and upon beast"
                              (Exo. 8:16-18)

LIMITATION OF BOGUS POWERS

Pharaoh and the people of Egypt did not know that with the manifestation of frogs, the metaphysical powers of the wise men came to their wits' end and the limit to which they can go. Here the limitation of metaphysical powers became evident, for these powers could no longer duplicate the miracles of the Power of Jehovah God via Moses.

When the limited powers of the wise men of Egypt could no longer perform, the limitless Power of the Most High God continued even on a higher degree through Moses and his brother Aaron.

It is true that the magicians and sorcerers of Egypt tried all they could to bring forth lice with all their

Behold I give unto you power

esoteric manipulations, but they could not. Surely they chanted higher occult "mantras", they invoked, they applied the highest esoteric techniques of their living avatar (Gopal Das), they projected and did all they could, yet they failed: *"And the magicians did so with their enchantments to bring forth lice, but they could not"*. Again Pharaoh was bamboozled, he was bewildered, for the greatest esoteric power of his avatar (man-made-god) had failed. Then came forth the Power of God on a higher dimension and chastised even the agents of the occult and esoteric powers.

> *"And they (Moses and Aaron) took ashes of the furnace, and sprinkled it up toward heaven; and it became a boil breaking forth with blains upon man, and upon beast. And the magicians could not stand before Moses because of the boils; for the boil was upon the magicians, and upon all the Egyptians"* **(Exo. 9:10, 11).**

The end of the highest invisible power within the metaphysical system of reality was a mere beginning of the Supreme Power of the spiritual system of reality. The god of Egypt came to naught whilst Moses waxed stronger and stronger via the potency of Jehovah and became a god to Pharaoh. The Power of God prevailed and plunged the magicians into predicament, through the painful boils that came upon them. From here the Power above powers waxed stronger to the extent that the whole Egypt was almost destroyed.

The highest power

THE MASTER KEY

This treaties is designed to set the stage for the recognition of the true Power. Today I bear witness that the Power of God is real even as it was of old. There are practical testimonies all over the world to confirm this, to show that the Spirit of God is for ever alive and active.

Now the Spirit of God is the Master Key of the Highest Spiritual Power. When the Spirit of the Living God is operating through you, miracle must occur. When the Spirit of God is in motion, every other power must bow just as it was in the beginning. If you have the Spirit of God abiding in you, then you have the master key of the Highest Power.

Whosoever holds the master key of Spiritual Power knows it. The master key of the Spiritual Power of the Universe is with me. This is no joke! The Lord has already given this Power to all His true servants, prophets and saints. If you can't practically demonstrate this Power already given, it is because you have not stretched forth your hand to receive.

> *"Behold, I give unto you power to tread on serpents and scorpions, and over all the power of the enemy: and nothing shall by any means hurt you"* **(Luke 10:19).**

Behold I give unto you power

> *"Verily I say unto you, whatsoever ye shall bind on earth shall be bound in heaven: and whatsoever ye shall loose on earth shall be loosed in heaven"* **(Matt. 18: 18).**

I give thanks and praises to the Lord who called me to partake in the movement of His Great Spirit towards the spiritual liberation of the earthmen. He has used me to bring the dead back to life; He has used me to give children to those seeking fruits of the womb; He has used me to heal the sick; He has used me to restore broken marriages; He has used me to bring several wizards, occultists and agents of darkness to the Lord Jesus Christ; He has used me to bless businesses and bring promotion; above all He has used me to revive many lives for Christ and bring salvation to many, among other manifestations of His true power. I know therefore and bear witness to this end, that the Power of God is real. Nothing is impossible with His Power!

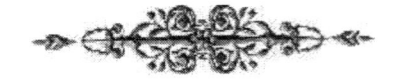

CHAPTER 4

POWER FOR VICTORY

"See, I have this day set thee over the nations and over the kingdoms, to root out, and to pull down, and to destroy, and to throw down, to build, and to plant."
(Jer. 1: 10)

QUESTION
How do you intend to begin your message on this topic, Behold I Give Unto You Power?

First of all, I think Bible students are aware that this topic is taken from the direct words of Our Lord Jesus Christ. In our text of discourse **(Luke 10:19),** the Lord said among other things: *"Behold, I give unto you power to tread on serpents and scorpions..."* Therefore let me begin by saying categorically, based on the words of Christ, that 'serpents and scorpions' are in existence. I also say this based on my past experience.

QUESTION
When the Lord spoke of *'serpents and scorpions'*, **what actually was He referring to?**

"Serpents and scorpions" in this connection refer to the empire of the powers of darkness, such as negative spirits and human agents operating under the Prince of Darkness. Consequently, *"serpents and scorpions"* represent witchcraft spirits and their human agents (witches and wizards), demons, psychic entities of the realm of darkness, invisible servants and elements of the vicious occult, controlling deities of the dark powers, principal esoteric powers, ascended masters and grand master of the vicious Astral system, mighty disembodied entities and arch spirits of the satanic world. Also included here are all the occult powers used by some men, women, boys, girls and children, in their direct and indirect spiritual warfare against their fellow human beings, whether through charms, amulets, or talisman.

QUESTION
What do you expect the reader of this message to achieve from all that you have to say on the subject matter of God's Power?

It is my sincere desire for the Spirit of God to use this Message to bring people to the consummate awareness and recognition of the true Power of God in their lives. Without this Supreme Power, which is found through Christ, no earthman can overcome the evil ones in the field of spiritual battle.

Remember that when I speak of the true Power of God, I am speaking of the Highest Spiritual Power, the very Power which the Lord gave to believers to tread on all the powers of darkness. This was the same Power used by Moses, Daniel, Elijah, Noah, Peter, Paul and John, to mention but a few.

Now there are some people who only preach or talk of this Power. There are many who have heard or read of this Power. Yet there are those who apart from talking or reading of this Power, have experienced or are experiencing same. I speak of the Highest Power both from what I have personally experienced as well as from what I have heard or read from the Scriptures.

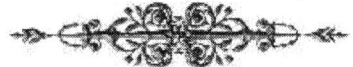

SERPENTS AND SCORPIONS

QUESTION
You said *'serpents and scorpions'* represent the powers of darkness. What would you say of the strength of these evil powers in a spiritual battle against a true child of God?

In our text of discourse **(Luke 10:19)** the Lord told His faithful followers, those living daily in the practical essence of the Holy Spirit, that they have the ultimate Power in God to tread on serpents and scorpions.

I believe that the faithful followers of the Lord are the true spiritual men on this planet. Such people may be many, they may be few, but surely they have spiritual Power to completely overcome, tread upon, subdue, bamboozle and discomfit all the powers of darkness in the field of spiritual warfare. This is the bona-fide spiritual platform wherein each and every believer should stand.

Remember the Words of the Lord: He made it clear that the Power given by Him to believers is for us not only to tread on serpents and scorpions, but that through this Power the believer will also tread *"OVER ALL THE POWER OF THE ENEMY"*. This is very important. The Lord did not say that believers have power over 'some' or over 'many' powers of the enemy.

The understanding here is that, it does not matter whatever is the degree of the powers of darkness, the believer has the absolute Power in God to overcome them all. To this end, even the highest power of the Prince of Darkness is under the feet of a true child of God in the name of Christ.

QUESTION
What would you say to a believers that is under the games of the powers of darkness?

Let such a believer rise in the strength of the Spirit of God and overcome all that is of darkness, for Christ has made him capable of this through His Blood.

It is true that the powers of darkness play diverse games against the true children of God in the field of spiritual warfare. But if you are strong in the Lord and in the power of His might, you will surely be victorious over all the games, crafts and manipulations of darkness. A true believer should know that there is no attack of the powers of darkness which Jesus Christ can not overcome for him. The Power of God has never and can never fail.

THE POWER OF VICTORY

QUESTION
Can you confirm what you are saying with a practical (personal) experience?

I have experienced and still experiencing the Power of God by the grace of the Lord. And I want to say that in times like this, we need the practical demonstration of the Power of God. It is the Power of God that makes the difference and gives us daily victory to live in Christ. The Lord has used me to manifest this Power in diverse ways.

RESTORATION OF WORK

For instance, Brother Napoleon Obi of 19, Ogunu Village Warri, Nigeria, went to work with the zeal to work effectively, though he had symptoms of malaria. Little did he know that the enemy wants to use his health condition to rob him of his job.

However, he survived the first-half of the day's job and went home on break. On reaching home, he became so tired and weak as a result of the malaria. Then he complained to his wife. But for the fact that he did not seek for permission in his office, and the hospital card which he would use to consult the company's doctor was in the office, he then managed to return to the office.

On reaching the office, the officer who was to sign his hospital card was out of reach. He decided to wait for him. During this period he fell asleep, and before he realized the game of the enemy, he was woken up by his boss, who became angry and inspite of his plea, stood firm on the

Power for victory

decision to terminate Brother Napoleon's employment.

Exercising his authority as the company's supervisor, he collected brother Napoleon's identity card and other documents, instructing that our brother should come the following day to collect his pay-off. It was under this condition that brother Napoleon came to me, to seek help from the Power of God. He later testified of his condition (under which he came to me) thus:

> "When all hope was lost, as my supervisor refused to change his mind, I now went to our Lord's Harbinger, who speaks in the mighty strength of God's Power. I thank God that this man of God was then holding a revival programme in Warri."

When brother Napoleon came, he told me all that happened to him in the office. As he was speaking, the Spirit of God opened my eyes and I saw an entity of the realm of darkness attempting to pull our brother out of a chair. Then an Angel of God appeared and banished the entity. I discovered that this negative spirit was invoked by a neighbor of brother Napoleon Obi. As I was about to pray for our brother, the Spirit of God said to me:

> *"Son of man, proclaim the decree of your Lord, and say to Napoleon: Behold, your work is restored back to you; and you will testify of this tomorrow. Harbinger, bear*

Behold I give unto you power

witness of this, for I am the Lord your God."

Then I proclaimed the decree of the Lord upon brother Napoleon, as I received from above. (As a messenger of God, I speak just as I receive from Him). Brother Napoleon truly believed the decree of the Lord upon him and went home in peace.

For one to receive from the *'Throne of Grace'*, he must have absolute faith in the Words of the Almighty God. Remember, '*without faith it is impossible to please God*' **(Heb. 11:6)**. You must believe in the Words of the Lord your God: whether it is the Words of God found in the Holy Scriptures, or the Words spoken now by Him directly to you or through His Prophet; without faith in God you can not receive the required Power of Victory. The Scripture says:

> "...*believe in the LORD your God, so shall ye be established; believe His prophets, so shall ye prosper*"   (2 Chro. 20 : 20).

I have already said that brother Napoleon Obi believed the decree of the Lord upon him. I specifically told him in the name of the Lord, that the following day he will return from his office with a testimony of victory. And it was so.

For it came to pass the following day that the person most senior to the supervisor came for a special visit from the head-office. When he heard of the matter of

Power for victory

brother Napoleon, by the working of the Spirit of God, he directed there and then that our brother should resume work immediately.

This is how the Power of God works. One is expected to have absolute confidence or unquestionable faith in this Supreme Power if he wants the Lord to fight for him. And when the Power of God begins to fight for you, not only that your victory is sure, but the Lord may even cause your adversaries to go into captivity. If you are a true believer, then you should learn how to allow God to fight for you always. God never disappoints. The Scripture says:

> *"Therefore all they that devour thee, shall be devoured; and all thine adversaries, everyone of them, shall go into captivity; and they that spoil thee shall be a spoil, and all that prey upon thee will I give for a prey"* (Jer. 30: 16).

HOW GOD SPEAKS TO ME

QUESTION
As the Harbinger of the Last Covenant in this generation, how does the Lord speak to you?

Generally speaking, God speaks to me through the Holy Scriptures as well as by the Spirit of God in me, which I am, which every man is. He also speaks to me through my fellow man and through diverse creatures in the physical world. God has been speaking to me also in the dream, revelation and other related spiritual experience via the Angels.

Specifically speaking, however, the Omnipresent Spirit of God has been speaking to me directly. Consequently, Jesus Christ has appeared and spoken to me several times both physically and in my dreams/revelations. Some times He opens my eyes to see Him without giving the same ability to those around me at that particular moment.

Furthermore, I bear witness from my own experience that the Power of God is real. For example, I do often hear the Lord speak clearly to me from my right ear. He speaks to me some times with the voice of the earthman; some times I hear Him speak like the mighty wave of the sea; some times He speaks to me like the voice of multitudes. It is true to me therefore that the Lord still speaks today as He did in the past, probably even more.

Power for victory

INVISIBLE WARFARE

QUESTION
You were formerly a Grand master of the occult and now a true messenger of Christ. From your past and present experiences, what would you say to human beings on the issue of spiritual warfare?

I want to say it again and again that there is an invisible spiritual warfare going on in this planet. I am in a spiritual battle. Each and everyone is in a spiritual battle, directly or indirectly, whether you know it or not. We all need the highest Power of the Almighty God to overcome the wicked spirits of darkness and their human agents. This is the Power which one can receive through Christ - Lord of Host!

It is true that in the past I took active part in the circle of Grand Masters to promote and sustain the manipulations of the empire of *'serpents and scorpions'* world-wide. The existence of the powers of darkness in itself, including their daily operation, in the light of the fact that the Lord gave us Power to tread on them, is enough to show that there is a spiritual warfare in this world. This is so because the Power He gave is exercised in a battle process.

One should not pass over this thought lightly. Remember I am speaking because I was with them. I am saying it categorically, based on my past experience and on the evidence of the Scriptures, that the Earth is a constant field of invisible warfare. Saint Paul wrote:

> *"For we wrestle not against flesh and blood, but against principalities, against powers, against the rulers of the darkness of this world, against spiritual wickedness in high places"* **(Eph. 6 : 12).**

The entities mentioned in this verse are the enemies of man. They are the proclaimed serpents and scorpions spoken of by Our Lord Jesus Christ. The children of men are under the constant invisible warfare of these entities. Without the Power of God which Christ gives, the earthman is nothing before the huge number of these wicked spirits. That is why the Scripture advised, that *we should be strong in the Lord and in the Power of His might.* **(See Eph. 6:10, 11).** We should strive to do this always, not a situation in which we are strong today and weak tomorrow. That can not help anyone.

QUESTION
Please could you throw more light on the activities of *'serpents and scorpions'* in their spiritual warfare against human beings?

The manipulation of the powers of darkness against

the earthmen is multidimensional. For instance, the powers of darkness may be manipulating a man to do the things he would not want to do, so as to put him in trouble. The powers of darkness may be working against you in diverse ways in your office (place of work), school, business and much more, through the vicious occult net-work of their human agents.

The powers of darkness may come against your spiritual life by manipulating and subjugating you via the force of iniquity. They may come against your finance with unnecessary expenses. Even one's health may come under serious spiritual attack of the negative spirits. Now marriage is also very important in this regard. To this end, the powers of darkness may come against your marriage life. To some unmarried men and women, they will make it difficult for them to marry; to some married men and women, they will manipulate them to see the evil and not the good in themselves.

This manipulation is designed to promote hatred, thus, separation. We truly need the Power above powers to completely overcome these and other manipulations of the proclaimed 'serpents and scorpions'. We need to put on the whole armour of God, for it is written:

> *"Finally, my brethren, be strong in the Lard and in the power of his might. Put on the whole armour of God, that ye may be able to stand against the wiles of the devil"*

Behold I give unto you power

CHAPTER 5

STRONGHOLD OF TRUE POWER

(Eph..6)

"How should one chase a thousand, and two put ten thousand to flight, except their Rock had sold them, and the LORD had shut them up?". (Deut. 32:30)

QUESTION
When you said that 'marriage is very important in this regard', do you mean to the powers of darkness?

Marriage is very important as far as the Spirit of God is concerned. It is a major point of contact for the manifestation of victory in spiritual warfare and blessings from the Lord. True marriage is a stronghold of the Power of God. The powers of darkness and their principal human agents know this very well, that is why they project several vicious psychic powers to frustrate successful marriages in different parts of the world.

QUESTION
In what way does marriage serve as a point of contact for the manifestation of victory and blessings from God?

First of all, in the beginning God created all things, and for each of His creation it is written: "*and God saw that it was good*". But there was only one situation out of the whole creation which was said not to be good. Thus it is written:

> "*And the Lord God said, it is not good that the man should be alone; I will make him an help meet for him*"   (Gen. 2:18).

When God saw that it is not good for man to be alone, He did not just give man a friend, sister, mother, father, or a child; but He gave him a wife as his help mate. This wife therefore was ordained to become his lover, sister, mother, friend and above all 'the bone of his bones and the flesh of his flesh.

Consequently, the man and his wife were expected by God to live in perfect love, unity, peace and reciprocal respect. This is the true marriage set forth by the Spirit of God. Anything contrary to this, is the marriage of 'cats and dogs'. The marriage of 'cats and dogs' enjoys the approval of the Prince of Darkness, because it is bereft of true love, unity, peace and respect. You only endure not enjoy such a marriage of animal propensities.

When you uphold true love in marriage, you manifest true agreement and unity. Unity is a stronghold and a major point of contact in receiving from the Lord. To this end, it is not good for you to be alone. It is even said: *"woe to him that is alone"*. **(See Eccl. 4:9-11).** And remember the Words of Our Lord Jesus Christ:

THE POWER OF UNITY

"Again I say unto you, that if two of you shall agree on earth as touching any thing that they shall ask, it shall be done for them of my Father which is in heaven"

(Matt. 18:19).

He did not say if three, four, ten or more shall agree; rather He said if two of you shall agree. And remember that the closest two people on earth is a man and his wife. I am not speaking of a man and his wives, but of one man and one wife. It is only in true marriage that one plus one is said to be one. In the ordinary sense, one plus one equals to two. But true marriage transcends the ordinary level, hence one plus one equals to one in marriage, based on love.

"Therefore shall a man leave his father and his mother, and shall cleave unto his wife: and they shall be one flesh"

Stronghold of true power

(Gen.2:24).

The Scripture further says that one shall chase a thousand and two shall chase ten thousand. It means that the blessings of God and His victory in the field of battle are in geometric progression and accelerated via the unity of two people in contact with the Spirit of God. Here true marriage serves as a major point of contact to quicken the aforementioned victory and blessings.

In other words, any relationship (marriage) sustained by the Holy Spirit in the practical sense, is a channel for the manifestation of the Power of God towards the frustration of the manipulations of the powers of darkness. The higher entities of the realm of darkness are aware of this. They are aware that the spiritual agreement of two children of God on Earth greatly defeats their strongholds.

That is why they are out to fight against true marriage in diverse ways. If you allow them to tamper with your marriage, they will come in and destroy the foundation of your Spiritual Power in that marriage (true love, unity, peace and respect). When this is done, the Power of God ceases to flow through your marriage, and the enemies will rejoice for blocking a channel of the Power of Light against them. That is why I said that marriage is very important towards our victory and blessings from God.

KNOWING THE TRUTH

QUESTION
The point you have made is very clear. But in the sense that a man is one only with his wife and not wives, what should those that have wives do? If a man comes to Christ, but has more than one wife, what should he do? This question is very important, because some churches teach that one should send away the rest of his wives apart from the first wife, while some teach otherwise. What is your opinion?

It is not a matter of my personal opinion, but of what the Lord says. My personal opinion may be invalid in the light of God's Word, whilst the Word of God is the ultimate reality.

There was a day in which a certain wealthy man in Lagos came for me to lead him to Christ. But the man came with his three wives. There was also something that he wanted the Lord to do for him. Then I began to think on a human level (personal opinion), according to my Scriptural understanding of the Will of God. I began to think that it would be proper for me to minister to the man on his problem only in the presence of his first wife, and that the rest two wives should not be there during the personal ministration on the man. This was after I had ministered on all of them, during which they gave their lives to the Lord. As I was thinking thus, I heard a mighty voice which said to me:

> *"Son of man, do the work of the Lord your God and leave the result to Me. And now hear, O son of man: If one comes with ten wives to serve Me, surely I will accept them. Therefore, say that they should live in peace, for all is well; and let them live for the Lord their God. If one comes to believe in your Lord, who does not believe at first, even with three of his wives, pronounce my peace upon them, for all is well. Behold, even with two wives, if they repent and believe in Me, I will surely receive them. But, son of man, if one who believes in Me, your Lord, takes a second wife while his first wife lives, behold, he has followed the path of adultery, for I will not receive him. Therefore, proclaim that whosoever believes in Me, but returns to take many wives, has the yoke of adultery upon him, even according to the number of women taken by him after his first wife".*

From what the Lord said to me, I learnt that He relates with people according to their respective situations. Therefore if an unbeliever comes to serve God with his wives, God will receive them. But if a believer leaves his first wife to marry another one, then he has done the wrong thing. However, I further learnt from the Lord that even the unbeliever who comes to serve Him with more than one wife, should live for the Lord (cease from having sex with them apart from his first wife). They can live together in peace and serve the Lord.

Even the believer who has one wife should strive also, at a certain stage, to give up sexual relationship with his wife and remain (as far as sex is concerned) as if he has no wife. Saint Paul wrote:

> *"But this I say, brethren, the time is short: It remaineth, that both they that have wives be as through they had none"* (Cor. 7:29).

How can one who has wife be as though he has none? The understanding here is not that you should send away your wife, or stop to live with her in the same house, or stop to feed and take care of her, or stop to love and cherish her. No, that is not the point here.

Rather when it is said that you should live with her as if you have no wife, that is on the sexual aspect. This is designed to enable you increase in the essence of God's Power. And it is necessary to uphold this injunction after having the number of children you want, and thus use the rest part of your life to cultivate complete divine service to the Lord. He promised to receive a new believer with his wives, but such a one, because he now believes, should strive also to uphold this principle. This principle is very important for spiritual development, though many of us do not preach it to the congregation

If you come to the Lord with many wives and continue to have sex with them, that is adultery for you. But without sex, you can live together as a family and serve the Lord. If you believe in the Lord, then any woman (wife or wives) you have sex with, apart from your first wife, is adultery. If your second wife (or more) can not stay without sexual relationship with you, she is free to go and marry another man who has not married before. God said a man and his wife, not a man and his wives, shall be one flesh.

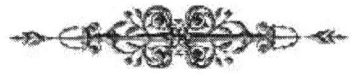

MARRIAGE RESTORATION VIA HIS POWER

QUESTION
So when the powers of darkness capture a particular marriage through their manipulations they destroy a major channel of the Power of God against the realm of darkness. But what happens when such a marriage is restored?

Let me share a testimony with you concerning a marriage that the Spirit of God restored and what happened thereafter. I am speaking of the marriage of

Behold I give unto you power

brother (Engr.) Danlami Nyazon, was the Senior Manager, Lines, NEPA Headquarters: 24/25 Marina, Lagos, Nigeria.

Before he came fully to the Lord, Danlami Nyazon left his family (wife and three children) and followed the women of the world, under the influence of negative powers. One of the women he followed was an agent of darkness. This agent of darkness finally took Danlami to different vicious occult centers, and the woman dominated the man with charms because the man sold himself to the wicked spirits via adultery.

When an agent of darkness gets you through food, through drinks, through fornication, or through adultery, the situation will become very tight for you. If the same agent gets you through more than one of these, you are gone, except the Power of God comes to set you free.

It was therefore under the occult and witchcraft manipulations of the woman agent of darkness, that brother Danlami forgot his wife and children and lived outside with the "daughters of Babylon". On some of the things he did during his sojourn to the world of iniquity, he later confessed as follows in a written brief testimony he sent to me:

> **"I rarely stayed at home to see to the welfare of my wife and children. I slept with women, took to heavy drinking of**

alcohol, became addicted to tobacco and could hardly go through a day without committing adultery. I also visited many native doctors, occultists and wizards for spiritual help. But the more I visited them, the more greater confusion sets in".

While this was going on, his wife, sister Grace Nyazon, continued to seek help from the Lord as a child of God. Though on a human level it was really a difficult period of her life. She expressed what she passed through then in her testimony, saying:

"He abandoned me and the children and took solace in the women outside. During this period I became a laughing stock and an object of ridicule. Indeed I experienced the most darkest part of my life, and the marriage became a burden to me".

For some years sister Grace lost contact with her husband. It was under this condition that she wrote me a letter after reading my book entitled OCCULT GRAND MASTER NOW IN CHRIST. In her letter she expressed her faith that the Spirit of God will help her through me. She confessed her faith in the limitless Power of the Lord of Hosts and Saviour of the world - Christ.

Behold I give unto you power

Her letter was among the multitudes of letters that came to me at that time. As I ended reading her letter, the mighty voice of the Lord spoke to me arid said:

"Harbinger and son of man, verily my Power is upon thee to destroy the yoke of the wicked. Therefore by your handshake with Danlami shall my Spirit come upon him, and the yoke shall be destroyed. And it shall come to pass, O ye Harbinger, that your Lord will set him free. Son of man, behold, Dalanmi shall return to himself, to his wife and children, even to the Lord his God. Then shall My Spirit cause him to be strengthened in the work of my Kingdom".

When the Lord speaks, it must come to pass. Therefore when the Lord spoke to me concerning the marriage of Mr. and Mrs. Nyazon, I knew that it must surely come to pass as decreed by the Lord. To this end, while in Lagos I sent for sister Grace Nyazon, using her address in the letter she wrote me. She came and was very happy that through her letter I could make out time to send for her.

It was not me that made out time to see her, rather it was the time of God for her victory. I have no time of my own. I only follow the time set out for me by my Lord whom I serve. It was the Will of God, the time of God, for me to see our sister. A true servant must obey the will of his master. I am nothing but a servant of servants of those who serve the feet of Christ!

However, I also sent for brother Danlami through his office address that the wife gave me. And by the special grace of God, by the Will of the Almighty, by the miracle of Jesus Christ, the Spirit of God touched his heart and he came to me.

When Brother Danlami came, I welcomed him. I pronounced the Peace of Christ upon him. And as soon as I shook hands with him, the Spirit of God came upon him. All the negative spirits that followed him fled. For darkness must flee from light. At that moment the Power of Our Lord manifested and the yoke of the enemy upon him was destroyed. Remember the Words of the Lord:

> *"And it shall come to pass in that day, that his burden shall be taken away from off thy shoulder, and his yoke from off thy neck, and the yoke shall be destroyed because of the anointing"* **(Isa. 10:27)**.

Surely the yoke of the Prince of Darkness is always destroyed by the anointing - the Highest Power of the Almighty God. This happened in the life of brother Danlami. It was that day that the man returned back to his wife after over three years in which he left his family. That day the man and his wife met face to face, and when

Behold I give unto you power

the Power of God came down they embraced and wept upon each other's arms.

That day the man repented and confessed his sins to the Lord, thus he was forgiven. For it is written: *"If we confess our sins, he is faithful and just to forgive us our sins, and to cleanse us from all unrighteousness"* (**1 John 1:9**). The Word of God came again to me, and the man was warned not to return to the path of iniquity. He gave his life fully to Christ and went home together with his wife.

Since then, as spoken to me by the Lord, brother Danlami has remained active in the work of the Lord his God. He is now highly committed to several outreach programmes through which many souls have come to the Lord. The Spirit of God has also used him and his wife to restore many broken homes (marriages) to the glory of God. And of what the Lord did for her, sister Grace Nyazon also stated:

> "In answer to my prayer, God sent His Harbinger, Iyke Nathan Uzorma, to intervene and restore the family back to God. My family is now united in the perfect love of Christ. Those who knew us during our crisis will truly testify to this glorious reunion. Praise the Lord".

After his total deliverance by the Power of Our Lord

Stronghold of true power

Jesus Christ, brother Danlami and his wife went home as I said earlier. The next day, however, he had a spiritual experience in which the enemy came against him but the Lord gave him victory. Speaking of this experience, brother Danlami said:

> "After the ministration of the man of God (Iyke Nathan Uzorma), I had a morning devotion on the morning of the following day with my wife and children. After this devotion, I fell asleep. Then the evil spirit that had held me bound in iniquities manifested. The Spirit of God gave me the Power and I banished this spirit through the Blood of Jesus Christ. Though this demon tried to paralyse my right hand; but I defeated him by calling upon the Lord. My wife was awake and bears witness to this encounter".

CHANNELS OF HIS POWER

QUESTION
We bless the name of the Lord, for this is a clear manifestation of His Power. But in the ordinary sense, it is difficult to understand how such Power

could be demonstrated only through a hand-shake. What would you say therefore on how the Power of God manifests through human channel?

It is true that the Power of the Almighty is manifested in diverse ways through His human channels. Indeed when God wants to manifest His Power, He can do so through anything visible or invisible. For instance, God can manifest His Power through your eyes. Remember that Christ said: *"The light of the body is the eyes; if therefore thine eye be single, thy whole body shall be full of light"* **(Matt.6:22)**. If your eyes be single, that is, always focusing on the Lord, you will be full of light. And it is by this light that the Power of God manifests. This means that God can manifest His Power through your eyes.

To this end, you may focus your eyes on an agent of darkness, and the rays of the light of Christ could pass through your eyes to banish the negative powers of that agent. This could happen with or without your direct knowledge of it. But this, however, depends on the degree of the intensification of the Power of God within you. It is also true that agents of darkness do use their eyes as channels of spiritual attack against their fellow human beings. This I also did in the past in one way or the other.

The Power of God can also manifest through your hands. As a matter of fact, the hand of every true child of

God is a channel of manifestation of God's Power. To this end, God can use your hand to heal the sick. Every true believer has this Power: *"... they shall lay hands on the sick, and they shall recover"* **(Mark. 16: 18)**. Therefore it is not surprising that God used my handshake with brother Danlami to destroy the yoke of the enemy upon him.

Now, remember how God manifested His Power in Egypt through the rod of Moses. Thus we found in the Scripture how the evidence of the Power of God through that rod became irresistible. At first it was an ordinary rod, but when the Power of the God Almighty possessed it, it became an extraordinary rod.

Not only that, for God can even manifest His Power through your shadow. Remember how the Spirit of God manifested to heal the sick through the shadow of Saint Peter. God can manifest His Power through your clothes. He can do so through the olive oil, through the water, through the wind, through a child, through an animal, through your handkerchief, through the words of your mouth, through fire and through His servant, to mention but a few. Indeed God can use anything to manifest His Power if He wants to do so.

CHAPTER 6

BONA-FIDE CHANNEL OF POWER

"Therefore if thine enemy hunger, feed him; if he thirst, give him drink: for in so doing thou shalt heap coals of fire on his head" (Rom: 12:20).

QUESTION

It is often said that the powers of darkness can only attack you, or get hold of you, through someone who is close to you. How true is this? Again, what should be our attitude towards a human being through which the powers of darkness attack us?

It is not true that the powers of darkness 'can only attack' you through a close relation or associate. Whereas it is true that the evil powers do often fight you through human beings close to you, they can also fight you through other human channels who may not be physically close to you. Nevertheless, it is true that the powers of darkness can rise against you through your father, mother, friend, brother, sister, husband, wife, child, church member, or business associate, to mention but a few. The Scriptures say:

> *"For the son dishonoureth the father, the daughter riseth up against her mother, the daughter in law against her mother in law; a man's enemies are the men of his own house"* **(Micah 7:6).**

> *"And the brother shall deliver up the brother to death, and the father the child: and the children shall rise against their parents, and cause them to be put to death. And a man's foes shall be they of his own household"* **(Matt. 10:21,36).**

In the first place, however, the spiritual warfare of believers is not directed against our fellow human beings. Rather our warfare is specifically directed against invisible entities, or spirit beings of the realms of darkness. This is the truth which every believer must uphold. For it is written:

> *"Our fight is not with people. It is against the leaders and the powers and the spirits of darkness in the world. It is against the demon world that works in the heavens"* **(Eph. 6:12, New Life Version).**

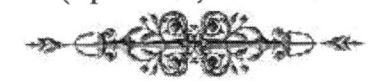

Behold I give unto you power

THE BANNER OF VICTORY

Therefore when the powers of darkness rise against you through your father, mother, child, friend, husband, wife, brother, sister, or neighbor, see beyond the workings of the human being involved and direct your spiritual warfare against the powers of darkness operating via the human entity.

At this point, you should in turn show your love, (the pure love of God), to each and every human being who is a direct or indirect channel of satanic attack against you. Whosoever is a channel of spiritual attack against you is of course your enemy in human terms. But if you must overcome the powers of darkness in the field of battle, you must love all your enemies in the world of man; you must pray for the good, not for the bad, of your enemies. Love is the essence of the Highest Power of God, and this Supreme Power surely belongs to you if you practically uphold love. To this end, Christ strongly admonished:

> *"Ye have heard that it hath been said, thou shalt love thy neighbour, and hate thine enemy. But I say unto you, love your enemies, bless them that curse you, do good to them that hate you, and pray for them which despitefully use you, and persecute you"* **(Math. 5 : 43, 44)**.

Bona-fide channel of power

The Power of the love of God is the banner of victory; and for as long as you remain faithful, true and worthy in the Holy Presence of Jesus Christ, you will continue to lift up this banner of victory in every field of battle. We are now living under a better covenant in which Christ is our perfect example, whilst we are commanded by Him to love our enemies. This is the sure path of victory. Therefore if you fail to uphold love in essence and in practice, you will be defeated in the field of spiritual warfare.

Often when the human channel of the attack of wicked spirits against you is identified, if you are not on the platform of the love of God, you may see yourself concentrating your thought, your prayer-energy, against such a human channel. This is a negative principle that can not help you gain victory as far as spiritual warfare is concerned.

Nevertheless, the fact remains that many attacks of the powers of darkness against you come through the human beings close to you. It may even come via the very person upon whom you rested your trust. This has been the process of attack of wicked spirits. It was in recognition of this that Our Lord Jesus Christ told the earthmen that *"a man's worst enemies will be right in his own home"* **(Math. 10:36, THE LIVING BIBLE, Paraphrased Self-Help Edition).**

Behold I give unto you power

From the teachings of Our Lord Jesus Christ, Lord and Saviour of the Universe, it is very clear that your foes (worst enemies) are right there in your home, in your household. Your home or household in this connection include the entire members of your family, the entire people of your village, all your neighbors and friends world-wide, all those working with you in the same establishment, the entire members of your mother's village, members of all the villages of your in-laws, all the members of your church or club, etc. In the field of invisible warfare, the enemies may rise against you through one or more of these.

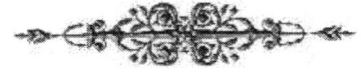

BETTER UNDERSTANDING

If you are a true child of God, your own part is always to love all men including all your enemies. Only by this can you manifest the true Power of God. **In Romans chapter 12 verse 20** Saint Paul wrote:

> *"Therefore if thine enemy hunger, feed him; if he thirst, give him drink: for in so doing thou shalt heap coals of fire on his head".*

Some of us have perverted the true essence of this ... used it to promote hatred instead of true love.

If while doing good to your enemy, you retain the thought that **"surely this my good will ultimately destroy him or heap coals of fire on him,"** then you have failed. Under this wrong thinking, after doing good to your enemy, you may begin to expect or to hear that certain evil or harm or even death has prevailed on him. This means that the main intention of your so-called "good work" was to project evil upon your enemy. This is a wrong path. It is not the path of Christ and does not uphold the message of Paul.

Paul did not mean that we should do good to our enemies with the intention of heaping coals of fire on them. The essence of his message is that each and every good you do to your enemy with pure love, without seeking any reward, and without the intention of heaping coals of fire on him, will backfire against your enemy, if he continues to do you evil while you are doing him good.

If you do good to your enemy with the intention that your good will harm him, you have failed before the Holy Spirit of God. It means that you did not forgive him in the first place and that you have grudge against him. That intention is grudge and lack of forgiveness. Anyone on the path of the Power of Jesus Christ must always forgive his enemy no matter the degree of the offence or how often the enemy offends him. If you want to be a channel through which the Power of God operates, you must not bear grudge against anyone, and you must

Behold I give unto you power

always forgive your enemies. To forgive is to be forgiven. Remember the Words of Christ: *"And forgive us our debts, as we forgive our debtors"* (Matt. 6: 12). The Lord further admonished:

> *"Therefore if thou bring thy gift to the altar, and there rememberest that thy brother hath aught against thee; Leave there thy gift before the alter, and go thy way; first be reconciled to thy brother, and then come and offer thy gift"* (Matt. 5:23, 24).

> *"And when ye stand praying, forgive, if ye have aught against any: that your Father also which is in heaven may forgive you your trespasses. But if ye do not forgive, neither will your Father which is in heaven forgive your trespasses"* (Mark 11:25, 26).

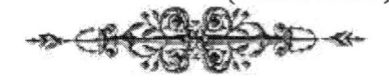

SPIRITUAL LESSON

QUESTION
Can you offer a practical example of how the good you do to your enemy could heap coals of fire on his head?

Bona-fide channel of power

The point is clear. Any good you do in love to one who continues to do you evil, will surely backfire on him, through the Universal Law of Reciprocal Action, which again is the Power of God in motion. If you do good in the essence of love, which is the true Power of God, to your enemy who continues to plot your down-fall, that enemy will never escape the judgment of the Living God. But if you have the intention that your good works will bring evil ultimately upon your enemy, that intention is grudge through which the Spirit of God will not work, meaning that your enemy will escape the coals of fire.

For example, there were two sisters of the same parents, from Delta State, Nigeria, who served simultaneously as matrons at the popular Eku Hospital. The senior one was a child of God who faithfully served Jesus Christ, while the younger one was an agent of darkness who camouflaged as a **'true church woman'**.

The elder sister truly loved her younger sister, and through her the younger one was employed to work at the hospital. Because of the way the elder sister behaved as a true child of God, she was loved the more by many people. This brought jealousy into the mind of the younger one. The jealousy did not just end in her mind because she went ahead and poisoned food for her sister. This still confirms the Words of Christ that *"a man's foes shall be they of his own household"*.

Before she brought **'the poisoned well prepared delicious food'** the Lord had revealed to the child of God not to eat any food brought to her by anyone within a space of time. She saw this in a dream because she had the gift of dreams and visions and was a full-time missionary in the Lord's Vineyard. To this end, she did not eat the food, rather she engaged in fasting and praying to the Lord her God.

Few days later, the younger sister became very sick. She paid evil for all the good done to her by her elder sister, therefore the Spirit of God heaped coals of fire on her head, whilst the sickness she planted against her sister with the powers of darkness, finally came upon her back to sender. Even while she was sick and admitted in the hospital, her elder sister was the very one who still took care of her. Of course the woman died, but before her death she openly confessed how she poisoned food for her elder sister. The woman was very surprised to hear that her **'beloved sister'** could do that to her. But she prayed for the Lord to forgive her and accept her into His Kingdom.

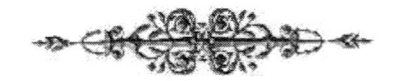

THE FINAL ORDER

QUESTION
What you are saying is that a true child of God must learn how to leave all matters in the hands of God?

Yes. Our Lord is the Perfect Manager of all the affairs of the great Universe. When God is fighting for you, when the Name and the Blood of Our Lord Jesus Christ is fighting for you, you must have victory. But a true child of God should never at any time revenge, fight back, or even pray against his human enemies.

Let me tell you this: The order of the Spirit of God is the final order. Any being in the Universe, be it spirit, angel, man, etc. that opposes His order, must go down in subjugation. For instance, when He directs that you should put up your hand, and you obey, then any one that rises against you must fall for your sake. For it is written:

> *"Ye are of God, little children, and have overcome them: because greater is he that is in you, than he that is in the world"*
> (1 John 4:4).

> *"Behold, they shall surely gather together, but not by me: whosoever shall gather together against thee shall fall for thy*

sake" (Isa.54:15).

When you are strong on the platform of the Power of God, all your enemies become nothing but channels of promotion and blessings to you. This is a spiritual fact based on the inexorable Will of God which is immutable. Your own part therefore is to love your enemies in the consummate understanding that they are spiritual channels through which you are blessed and lifted. That is why Christ said:

> *"Blessed are ye, when men shall hate you, and when they shall separate you from their company, and shall reproach you, and cast out your name as evil, for the Son of man's sake"* (Luke 6:22).

That is the point. You are truly blessed when men hate you for Christ sake. In other words, your enemies unknown to them serve as spiritual channels of your blessings. Remember how all the enemies of Joseph became the channels of his great blessings in Egypt. He became a Prime Minister in that land into which his enemies sold him as a slave. His enemies, however, were also members of his household. Even the false accusation of his master's wife brought blessings to him in the final analysis because through that, he was cast into prison and from prison he came to glory.

Therefore if you desire that all men should love you and speak well of you, you are indirectly desiring that the channels of your blessings be closed. Thus Christ said: *"Woe unto you, when all men shall speak well of you..."* **(Luke 6:26).** If you praise me, or speak well of me, you may think you are helping me. But I have to be very careful over such, so that I will not be carried away and go astray. But when you tell lies against me, or accuse me falsely, or plan evil against me, then I rejoice for God has opened a channel of blessings for me. If you accuse me falsely, even if you proclaim that I am not using the Power of God, I will not defend myself. Never! Because if I defend myself, I am working against my channel of blessings. You should realise that false accusation and speaking evil of you because of the Lord, can not destroy what God has planted. The Scripture says:

> *"Unless the LORD builds the house, those who build It labour in vain. Unless the LORD watches over the city, the watchman stays awake in vain"* **(Psalm 127:1, Revised Standard Version).**

CHAPTER 7

THE HIGH CRAFT OF DARKNESS

"... be strong in the Lord, and in the power of His might. Put on the whole armour of God, that ye may be able to stand against the wiles of the devil." (Eph. 6:10,11).

QUESTION
From your former experience in the realm of the occult and witchcraft, do the powers of darkness attack Pastors more than other Christians?

The powers of darkness have specific attack against all the shepherds in the Body of Christ. **In Matthew chapter 26 verse 31,** the Lord said: *"...smite the shepherd, and the sheep of the flock shall be scattered abroad".*

Though Christ spoke of what was written of Him, but this is the same process the powers of darkness follow to attack the people of God. When I speak of shepherds in this connection, I am speaking of all those who are called by God into His Vineyard as full-time ministers, as well as those who are called by God to lead others in one way

The high craft of darkness

or the other in the Body of Christ (who may not be full-time ministers). I am not speaking of one who wears collar without the call of God.

Now, each and every shepherd in the Body of Christ is a major target of the attack of the powers of darkness. When a shepherd is captured, the sheep will be scattered. Therefore the best way to get the sheep is to smite the shepherd. This is what the powers of darkness do. This was also the reason why the Prince of Darkness went to resist the High Priest of God, as recorded in **Zachariah chapter 3 verses 1 and 2:**

> *"And he shewed me Joshua the high Priest standing before the angel of the LORD, and Satan standing at his right hand to resist him. And the LORD said unto Satan, the LORD rebuke thee, O Satan; even the LORD that hath chosen Jerusalem rebuke thee..."*

You can now better understand what I am saying. Here the High Priest Joshua was in the Holy Presence of God to receive from Him for the entire Israel, then the Prince of Darkness appeared to resist the High Priest. The High Priest was a shepherd of the people of God. As he came into the Presence of God, the Great Lord sent His Angel to him; thus he was seen standing before the Angel of the Lord.

Behold I give unto you power

Surely the Angel of the Lord came with great blessings from God. The blessings of God include peace, health, victory, power, wealth, joy and righteousness, to mention but a few. These and much more were to be passed to the people of God by the Angel via the High Priest. The High Priest as a shepherd of God's people, stood before the Angel on behalf of the whole Israel. This is the duty of every true shepherd.

Then Satan came. The Prince of Darkness did not want the blessings from God to reach the people of Israel. He knew that the best way to do this, is not by sending his vicious spirits from house to house tempting the people of God to hinder their blessings. Whereas the powers of darkness do this, they know that the best way to hinder the blessings of the people of God is to prevent a shepherd from receiving from God in this regard.

This was why Satan went to resist the High Priest. He wanted to cut-off the free flow of the blessings of God to Israel. And if he defeats the High Priest, it means he had defeated the blessings of the entire people of God. This is what every true shepherd should know. A true shepherd is the one made by God for man, not the one made by man for man. To this end, when you recognize a true shepherd, please give him spiritual and material support, because he stands for you

WHY SOME SHEPHERDS LACK POWER

QUESTION
Does it mean also that the Power of God is given more to the shepherds than the rest of the people of God? And how do we recognize a true shepherd?

In the first place it is said that to whom much is given, much is required. All true believers in Christ live in the essence of the Power of God. But even on this spiritual platform, all men are not on the same level. There are diverse levels in the realm of Spiritual Power.

Now listen to this illustration: There was a certain wise man who, however, was used to licking sweets. I call him 'wise man' because every child of God is a wise man. Christ even told us to be as wise as serpents. This wise man (shepherd), or man of God, had the Power to speak in the name of God, and whatever he says comes to pass.

In that same city, there was a little girl who was always stealing her mother's money to buy sweets, because she was addicted to sweet. One day her mother brought her to the man of God, so he could speak the Word of Power and stop her child from licking sweets. But the wise man did not speak as expected, rather he told the woman to go and come back with the girl after seven days.

The woman did not understand why the wise man

failed to speak the Word of Power that day. However, she left with her child still. From that very day, the wise man stopped licking sweets. He knew that there is no way the Power of the Lord will use him to stop another person from licking sweets, whereas he himself was addicted to sweets. After seven days the woman returned again with her girl, and when the wise man spoke the Word of Power, the little girl stopped licking sweet from that day. This is how the Spirit of God works (Those who have ears to hear, let them hear).

Now, on how to recognize a true shepherd: there are certain basic principles in this regard. Specifically, a true shepherd must lead by example. He must be a sober and humble person, who can tolerate or control the urge to speak, the mind's demands, the actions of anger and the urges of the tongue, belly and genitals. One who is bereft of these, is not spiritually qualified to lead others, neither is he qualified to be led by the Lord.

TITLE VIS-A-VIS POWER

QUESTION
One thing is not yet clear to me. Please I want you to be specific. I want to know if Pastors and Bishops, for instance, have more Power of God than those under them?

The high craft of darkness

This may or may not be the case. First of all, practical demonstration of God's Power has nothing to do with mere religious titles. Demonstration of Spiritual Power has nothing to do with having such titles as Elder, Bishop, Deacon, Pastor, Apostle, Evangelist, Pope or Reverend, to mention but a few. These titles are good for the smooth administration of the work of God on Earth. But when it comes to the aspect of the practical demonstration of Power, these titles in themselves do not matter.

In the field of spiritual warfare, the yoke of the Prince of Darkness is destroyed because of the anointing, not because of the title. **(See Isaiah 10:27)**. This is the truth of the matter. Therefore if a shepherd has more Spiritual Power than those under him, it is because of the anointing of God upon him and not because of his title. But today it appears that some of us are more interested in big religious titles than the anointing of the Supreme Power.

The Spiritual Power of the Lord is the only real Power. It is the Highest Power. I have already said that this Power does not operate via religious titles but on the level of your anointing. There are only two major titles for all the children of God on Earth - **'Brother' or 'Sister'**.

If you experience the presence or the radiant Vicinity of Our Lord Jesus Christ in the realms beyond, as I am privileged to experience, you will learn in that Supreme Abode of the multidimensional God that, in this world of man, no believer is recognized as Pope, Apostle, Bishop, Evangelist, Pastor, etc. I learnt directly from Him that you are either a brother or sister.

In other words, you may have religious title without the Power of God. You may also have religious title and at the same time possess Spiritual Power. But the Power of God possessed by you in this connection is not on the strength of your religious title. We must understand that Spiritual Power is completely independent and absolutely beyond all religious titles.

One day, during a major crusade involving more than thirty five different church denominations, in which I was the guest speaker, I was introduced to the crowd with my several past occult titles, with a specific proclamation of my present as a great man of God. After this introduction, the expectation of the people was that 'a great man of God' has come.

Little did I know that many of those present had removed their faith from the Living God and focused on me - the mortal man. This is very dangerous for both the speaker and the listener. It can not help a speaker or listener make the required progress on the path of the Lord. It leads to vanity, which is one of the major channels of psychic attack. And as I was being introduced to the crowd at that time, the Lord spoke to me like the wave of the sea, saying:

> *"Son of man, behold, the hearts of the children of men are turned even unto the multitude of that given this day to you by men as titles. But thou shall not speak to them on the strength of these. Speak and warn them for me, O Harbinger of the Last Covenant, that woe comes to he whose heart is departed from Me. And now, son of man, proclaim that your Lord is your strength; for behold, I am the Source of endless power, love and knowledge; I am the Lord thy God".*

When I heard these I bowed on the floor to the Lord before the people and worshipped the Almighty who lives for ever and ever. At that moment also, as I stood up to speak, I informed the crowd that in the light of the reality of the Holy Spirit, all the great titles given to me before them are invalid and should not be seen as the basis by which the Lord will pass through me to minister. Then I ministered in the mighty name of the Lord and it was well. That night the Spirit of God moved mightily and men received salvation, deliverance, healing and great blessings from the Living God.

Some of us often run after big religious titles. But the Power of God does not operate that way. Our Lord once said: *"... the harvest truly is plenteous, but the labourers*

Behold I give unto you power

are few" (**Matt. 9:37**). The labourers in this connection are not just those who have religious titles. The labourers specifically are those filled with the Holy Spirit who serve as the true channels of the manifestation of His Almighty Power. This can be anyone - boy, girl, child, man, woman, bishop, pastor etc. But it must be someone who lives in the consummate essence of the Light of Jesus Christ.

HIS SEAL AND RECOGNITION OF POWER

QUESTION

In **Philippians** chapter 2 verse 10, it is written *"That at the name of Jesus every knee should bow, of things in heaven, and things in earth, and things under the earth"*. How do you understand this verse, in the light of the fact that there are some spirits that appear to be stubborn even at the mention of the name of Jesus Christ?

Let me make this point clear: the idea of shouting "Jesus! Jesus!!" without His SEAL and RECOGNITION, may not help anyone in the field of spiritual warfare. His seal is His Blood, without which we can not overcome; while His recognition is the Spirit of Righteousness operating in us, that is THE SPIRIT OF CHRIST.

The high craft of darkness

Remember the case of the seven sons of Sceva. They were the children of a chief of the priests of God. They used the name of Jesus Christ in their spiritual warfare against the powers of darkness, yet they were completely defeated in the field of spiritual battle. This is the point we should bear in mind, that if you don't have the seal and recognition of Christ upon your life, the powers of darkness will not obey your command even if you shout the name of Jesus:

> *"Then certain of the vagabond Jews, exorcists, took upon them to call over them which had evil spirits the name of the Lord Jesus, saying, we adjure you by Jesus whom Paul preacheth. And there were seven sons of one Sceva, a Jew, and chief of the Priests, which did so. And the evil spirit answered and said, Jesus I know, and Paul I know; but who are ye? And the man in whom the evil spirit was leaped on them, and overcame them, and prevailed against them, so that they fled out of that house naked and wounded"*
> **(Acts 19:13-16).**

It is true that at the name of Jesus Christ every knee must bow. Bowing at the name of Christ in this connection is different from obeying your command at the name of Jesus Christ in the field of spiritual warfare.

Behold I give unto you power

When it is said that every knee must bow at the name of Jesus Christ, it means that when the Spirit of God, the Power of Christ, is in motion, everything must bow to Him. It also means that the recognition of the everlasting potency of Our Lord Jesus Christ is Supreme and absolutely transcends the entire realms of matter, space, energy and time. For Christ is the Creator and Lord of the Universe. All spirits, angels, men, etc. are subjected to Him.

Nevertheless, for the powers of darkness to submit to the command of the earthman in the name of Jesus Christ, such a man must possess the Spirit of Christ in him. Without the Spirit of Christ in you, the Prince of Darkness and his wicked spirits will not obey your command in the name of Christ.

The Spirit of Christ in you upholds the seal of the Living God which is the Blood of the Lamb. The Spirit of Christ in you also upholds the recognition of the, Godhead via the righteousness, peace and joy of the Holy Spirit. Without these you are as empty as a "deaf-nut" in the field of spiritual warfare.

This was where the seven sons of Sceva failed. And this is where many of us have failed. The sons of Sceva did not have the Spirit of Christ in them. They were completely bereft of the divine protection of the Blood of the Lamb and His holiness. Thus they failed in the field of spiritual warfare, even though they called upon

The high craft of darkness

the name of Jesus Christ.

Remember that the sons of Sceva were the children of a priest of God. They truly heard the Word of God, for they heard Paul preaching the Power of Christ, yet they did not have the Spirit of Christ in them. Among the earthmen, the sons of Sceva were said to be members of the nation of God and the children of a chief of the priests of God. But spiritually they had no recognition. This manifested when they came face to face with the spirit of darkness and called upon the name of the Lord against the wicked spirit. Yet they failed. They are like some of us who think that merely by going to church, reading the Bible and calling upon Jesus we will overcome the powers of darkness.

When the evil spirit said *"Jesus I know"*, it means that the entire powers of darkness know that they are minor entities and bogus powers in the light of the multidimensional Power of Our Lord Jesus Christ. When the spirit also said: *"and Paul I know"*, it means that the powers of darkness know that Paul has the Spirit of Christ in him.

To this end, they knew that they must bow to Jesus Christ as the Lord of all that is, as well as to the Spiritual Authority of Christ operating in Paul. But the powers of darkness were not prepared to obey the command of the sons of Sceva, who did not fulfill the most vital principle of receiving help from Christ. They did not fulfill the condition which Christ Himself set forth when He said:

> *"If ye abide in me, and my words abide in you, ye shall ask what ye will, and it shall be done unto you"* **(John 15: 7)**.

This is the most bona-fide condition under which the name of the Lord will work for you. You must abide in Him and His Words must abide in you, then He will fight for you: that is to say, the Almighty Power inherent in His glorious name will then manifest for your victory over the Prince of Darkness. Here again the sons of Sceva failed, to the extent that they were even maimed in the battle field. Listen once again to what happened to them:

> *"And the man in whom the evil spirit was leaped on them, and overcame them, and prevailed against them, so that they fled out of that house naked and wounded".*

Do you think it is all that easy for you to rise from the "altar" of iniquity and then command the powers of darkness to flee in the name of Christ? I tell you the truth, they will not obey your command, except you repent first and seek the Lord your God.

Earthman, when you rise from the iniquity of deep hate against others, will evil spirits obey your command? Surely they will not obey you. When you are exasperated and filled with the thoughts of vanity and attachment to mundane things, the evil ones will surely prevail against you.

When you have not given your life fully to Jesus Christ, that is when the Spirit of Christ is not in you, let it be known to you that the powers of darkness shall by no means obey your spiritual command. When the Prince of Darkness comes and finds that you don't have the seal of the Blood of the Lamb upon your life, he then knows that you have no portion of victory on the path of the Father.

THE BLOOD OF JESUS CHRIST

QUESTION
You have spoken of the Blood of Christ as our seal of victory. This is an absolute spiritual fact. But can you throw more light on this for the benefit of others?

It is a mystery, yet it is true, that the Highest Spiritual Power of the Almighty God operates for our victory in this world of man through the Blood of Our Lord Jesus Christ. No man on Earth today can possess or manifest the true Power of God without the Blood of Christ.

It was by His Blood that the Lord of Hosts, in His

Behold I give unto you power

disguised role as THE SON OF MAN, crushed the Prince of Darkness on the cross for the salvation of the earthman, and for the daily victory of all the children of God world-wide.

'Blood', however, is very important, both for the kingdom of God and for the realms of darkness. For instance, the blood of the children of men enables the wicked spirits to advance the manipulations of the Prince of Darkness in diverse ways. Witches and wizards are prominent in this regard. Even the blood of beasts and birds also help in one way or the other to promote diverse rituals of the occult system.

On the path of the Holy Kingdom of the Living God, **'Blood'** is also very important whilst the Blood of THE SON OF MAN, (Our Lord Jesus Christ) is the final seal of the Power of the Godhead above and beneath. Seekers of the true Power of God will do nothing more than to uphold the last seal of true Power - the Blood of Our Lord Jesus Christ!

Furthermore, the spiritual path to the Almighty God based on the foundation laid via the Blood of Jesus Christ, is the foremost bona-fide path of the spiritual system of reality. This path is the only sure way to God. Christ Himself also said:

> *"Verily, verily, I say unto you, He that entereth not by the door into the sheepfold,*

but climbeth up some other way, the same is a thief and a robber. Then said Jesus. unto them again, verily, verily, I say unto you, I am the door of the sheep"
(John 10:1, 7).

This simply means that any other path, no matter how great or small it may be, which is not based on the foundation of the Blood of Our Lord Jesus Christ, is a man-made path and can not lead man to the Holy Presence of the true God.

MAN-MADE PATH

Now, there are many man-made paths on Earth that are completely bereft of the Power of the God of Moses. There are many man-made religions in the world of man that are bogus in the light of the Divine Power of the Lord God Almighty. I have been speaking to the earthmen that we don't need a man-made religion (no matter how great), to cover the shame of our iniquities, rather we need the Blood of Christ to wash us clean. Now remember some of the things that took place immediately after the fall of Adam and Eve. **Genesis chapter 3 verse 7 and 21** reported that:

"And the eyes of them both were opened,

and they knew that they were naked; and they sewed fig leaves together, and made themselves aprons... Unto Adam also and to his wife did the LORD God make coats of skins, and clothed them".

When Adam and Eve fell and saw that they were naked before the Lord, the Bible says that they used fig leaves and made aprons for themselves. They made this to cover their nakedness. This apron was not made for them by the Lord, rather they made it for themselves. This is the symbol of the origin of all the man-made religions. There is a great difference between the religion made for man by man and the religion made by God for man.

God knew that the aprons made by Adam and Eve cannot cover their nakedness in His presence. Thus He made coats of skins for them. The coats of skins were made by God from the skins of beasts. Meaning that the blood of beasts was shed before their skins were used to make coats. This became the symbol of the true religion made by God for man, which is established upon the Blood of the Lamb - Jesus Christ. In other words, God took away from Adam and Eve their man-made religion of fig leaves and made for them the better religion (of the blood) to cover their nakedness.

Therefore I advise the earthman to do away with all forms of man-made religions; do away with all forms of

The high craft of darkness

fig-leave religions designed by your fellow men, whom you proclaim to be Masters, Prophets, Sages and Avatars, for your nakedness can not be covered by them. Receive the true garment of God, which is the Blood of the Lamb, that your nakedness may be covered, and for you to possess the everlasting salvation, grace and Power of the Most High God.

You don't need a fig-leave religion to cover up your iniquities. You don't need to attend a church so as to cover up your nefarious acts. Rather you need the Blood of Our Lord Jesus Christ to wash you clean. We all need the Power of God in times like this. But the true Power of the Lord comes through the foundation which Christ laid by His Perfect Blood.

CHAPTER 8

ALL THINGS ARE POSSIBLE

"But Jesus behold them, and said unto them, with men this is impossible; but with God all things are possible."
(Math. 19:26).

QUESTION
The Scripture says that all things are possible through prayers. Some people think that this is a mere consolation, because they have observed that there are certain things which their prayers have not made possible. From your own experience and understanding, do you believe that with God all things are possible?

Listen! It was Our Lord Jesus Christ Himself who directly proclaimed that *"with God all things are possible"* (**Math. 19:26**). The words of the Lord are the sole ultimate truth in all the realms of existence. I have personally received a message from the Lord on this very matter. One day, during my fasting and prayer, the Lord spoke to me on many matters of spiritual life, including the fact that all things are possible with Him.

On this very matter, He said to me:

> *"O Harbinger, know and understand that all things are possible with Me, your Lord! Behold, there is no impossibility when I set forth My Power to do a thing. Therefore whatever is the problem of the children of men, when they come to you, and if they believe in the Power of your Lord, call forth my Power to take control; and, behold, there must be a change for the better. O son of man, say to the children of men, that when the Power of your Lord comes into any venture, that venture must prevail by My Spirit. Say also, that there is no limitation, no impossibility, in the operation of the Spirit of thy Lord who makes all things possible".*

I bear witness to the faithful and the faithless, that these are the Words of the Lord. When you read the Bible, you will see many impossible things that became possible by the Power of God. But if you come to God with doubt, you will not receive from Him, not because all things are not possible with Him, but because of your unbelief. **(See James 1:5-8, Math. 17:14-21).**

Behold I give unto you power
BEYOND LIMITATION

I believe strongly that with God all things are possible. Let me share a testimony in this connection. In 1995 my wife, (then my fiancée), underwent the final examination in her Bachelor degree programme at the University of Benin. During the exam, there was a day in which she was to answer four questions in her course within a specific time. She was weak due to acute menstrual pain. However, she finished answering one question, and as she was about to start the second one, time was up. The subject was a **'core course'** that determines whether one will graduate or not. When this happened, she became sad and came that same day to tell me.

Then I prayed for her in the mighty name of the Lord. I knew that with the Lord all things are possible. I did not limit the Power of God by thinking that the exam is over and there is nothing God will do again about it at that instance. Rather I prayed to the Lord to help her. The moment I ended praying for her, I heard a voice which said to me:

"Son of man, know thou this that thy Lord has written and passed the examination for My daughter. Therefore say to her: surely the Lord of Hosts will send His Angel to write the answers to the rest of the questions you never wrote, that

you may bear witness of the Power of your Lord. Son of man, know thou also that I am the Supreme University; I am the Examiner; I am the True Teacher; behold, I am the Lord thy God".

When I heard these, I bowed on the ground and worshipped the Lord God Almighty. Then I spoke the Word of the Lord to her. Indeed she wondered at first how such a thing could be. But after receiving the Words of the Lord she believed and praised the Lord. When finally the result of this exam was released, she truly passed even the questions she never answered. For the Great Lord sent forth an Angel to write them for her, in fulfillment of His Words. This a practical demonstration of the fact that with God all things are possible. Often when the Power of God is demonstrated this way, some people wrongly think that the occult power did it. And I ask: is the occult power more powerful than Christ? God forbid. Personally I have several testimonies to show that there is no impossibility with God.

We must understand that the Spiritual Power of the Almighty God has no limit. Indeed the Supreme Power of the Almighty God has no limit in eternity. The Power of God is God Himself. It is the Power of God which created the Heavens and the Earth and all the known and unknown Universes. The Power of God operates in diverse forms in all the visible and the invisible realms of existence. Nevertheless, in all the realms of existence,

Behold I give unto you power

as well as the world of man, the Blood of Our Lord Jesus Christ is the foundation of the operation of the Almighty Power of God.

REVEALER OF SECRETS

The Power of God is also the revealer of secrets. And when this Power is operating through you or in you, the secrets of the earthmen shall not be hidden from you. One day in Lagos, Nigeria, a brother came to me with his wife. He had a problem which he wanted the Spirit of God to solve for him through me.

Consequently, this brother narrated his problem. According to him, he took his company's money to the bank on behalf of the company. While in the bank it was discovered that part of the money was missing. The brother told me categorically that he knew nothing about the missing money, but that his company suspended him because of it. He then came to seek help from the Lord, so that he will not be sacked but recalled by the Company.

As he was speaking, the Holy Spirit opened my eyes and I saw something like television through which I saw how the brother stole the money. Everything was played back by the Spirit of God for me to see. Then I realized

All things are possible

that the brother, who strongly claimed to be a **"born again"** Christian, was the very person who stole the money. At that moment I also heard a voice which said to me:

> *"Son of man, seek no blessing from Me, your Lord, for this hypocrite who seeks My Power in vain. For, behold, he seeks the help of your Lord even with multitude of falsehood. But, son of man, surely his lies before Me shall ruin him in the hand of the wasters, except he repents".*

Then I asked the man: **"Brother, are you telling me before the Lord that you know nothing about the missing money?"** He replied and said **"God forbid!** I have been in the Lord now for over fifteen years by His grace, and God is my witness that money has never made me to sin against Him. My wife is here. She can bear witness also that even while we were in the world, stealing was never a part of us." I said: **"Okay, let us pray"** As I laid hands on him to pray, I said:

> "O Lord of Hosts and Savior of the World; O my Lord the Omnipotent, You are powerful than fire. You said that the truth shall set us free. If this man has said the truth before You, I proclaim now that he is free even by Your Power given to me. But, O my Lord, if he has

told lies before You, he will surely be ruined in the hand of the wasters; as spoken by You, except he repents. Thank you Father, for you have heard even more than I have asked, through the name of Our Lord Jesus Christ, - Amen".

As soon as I ended the prayer, he became very uncomfortable. He immediately left with his wife and returned alone in about 20 minutes later. He came to repent and confess his sins. He then confessed that he truly stole the money, but he pleaded that he did not want his wife to know that he came back to confess.

However, the Lord directed that the man should go and bring his wife and let his confession also be before her if he wants true deliverance. The man did as the Lord directed. He came back with his wife and openly confessed his sins. Then the Lord empowered me to pray for God's mercy and victory upon him, which I did. Thereafter everything became well with him. God said that.

> *"If we say that we have no sin, we deceive ourselves, and the truth is not in us. If we confess our sins, he is faithful and just to forgive us our sins, and to cleanse us from all unrighteousness"* **(1 John 1:8-9).**

All things are possible

This is how God works. When that brother told lies, he placed himself outside the divine protection of Jesus Christ. This gave the powers of darkness right over him. But when he repented and confessed his sins, the Spirit of God returned to fight for him.

We are the ones who give the powers of darkness right over us - by placing ourselves outside the Power of God through the multitude of our iniquities. But when we confess our sins and forsake them, the Spirit of Light of the Living God comes to take control. Remember that when the Spirit of God is in control of your life, you must have the ultimate victory.

POWER IN CONFESSION

There was a couple that met me in Benin City, Nigeria. The woman had a problem - she was pregnant for two years and eight months. This prolonged pregnancy was the result of a spiritual attack by the powers of darkness. When they came to me to seek help from the Lord, the Holy Spirit opened my eyes to see the major cause of the problem and the way out of it.

I saw that this spiritual attack was made possible for the powers of darkness via the act of illicit sex (adultery) committed by her husband. The man had sex with three different women, whilst the problem came through one of the women who was an agent of darkness.

The moment the man had sex with that woman agent of darkness, the woman used the vicious spirits to contaminate the man's penis through the art of witchcraft. And when the man finally 'made love' to his wife few days later, the vicious spirits further advanced their manipulations to the extent that they dominated the woman's pregnancy for several months.

The couple went to different places and churches seeking for solution. But when they met me, the Spirit of God gave them solution. You may not get solution from a church, but you must get from the Spirit of God. A church where the Spirit of God operates must have the required solution. But a church bereft of the Spirit of God can do nothing to help you in the face of a spiritual attack.

Following what the Lord told me, I prayed for the couple and spoke to them in the same vein. I told them to go home and do one thing: the man was told to confess all his sins to God and to the hearing of his wife, after which the wife should sincerely pray for his forgiveness. Then the man will in turn pray for the wife, that the Lord should help her. They were told to do this in their house and come back to me within three days.

The woman was specifically told that if she fails to

All things are possible

forgive her husband after the confession, her problem will remain; but if she forgives him, the mercy of God will come down upon them to the extent that seven days shall not pass and she will deliver the child in her womb. Before that time the powers of darkness stole the child in her womb and replaced it with a 'psychic element'.

The couple traveled back to their station (Onitsha) and returned again to meet me as directed. But when they reached home, they did as they were commanded by the Lord through me. Indeed the man confessed his act of adultery to his wife whilst the woman sincerely forgave him and received prayer from him. When they came, I prayed for them again and set forth the decree of the Lord upon them.

Consequently, the woman delivered a baby boy five days later, by the Power of Jesus Christ! The Lord has made me to experience His Almighty Power in diverse forms, to show that there is no impossibility before Him.

RESTORATION POWER

There was a day in which some women brought the corpse of a fifteen year old boy to me. The boy, a child of God, died the previous night. His father traveled out of the city. The parents are also members of the family of

Behold I give unto you power

God. When they brought the corpse to me, I was not happy that they came with the corpse without any previous information or arrangement. I began to think with the mind of the earthman, that if I pray and the dead fails to come back to life, those that came will think that the Power of the Lord is not real. Then I decided to send them away with the corpse. But I went in to pray first and hear from the Lord. Then the Word of God came to me, and He said:

> *"Son of man, think not of the Power of they Lord with the limitation of the mind of the children of men. But think of thy Lord with the mind of My Divine Spirit, for there is no impossibility with Me, thy Lord. And now, O ye Harbinger of the last Covenant, bear witness this day of the Power of thy Lord to the faithful and the faithless"*

Then the Lord said several other things to me. He specifically directed that I should ask the mother of the boy to bathe the corpse in my bathroom and that I should anoint them thereafter. I was now convinced that the Lord will bring the dead boy back to life. I thought that the Lord will do this when I will anoint them. But it came to pass that as the woman was bathing her son, the boy came back to life, to the glory of the Father.

I learnt something very important from what the Lord

All things are possible

did that day. When the boy came back to life, people gathered to rejoice and praise the Lord. Among those present was Mr Godwin Osaji, Manager Union Bank, Oghara, Delta State, Nigeria. People were behaving and speaking as if I was the one who brought the dead back to life.

I told them the limitation of my human knowledge in this matter and of the limitless Power of Jehovah God and His Christ. I exposed everything that went on in my mind when they came - and how the Lord also proved to me through this miracle that without Him we can do nothing. Then many gave their lives to Christ.

We should never joke with the Power of the Living God. We should never doubt this Power. With God all things are possible! As children of God, we are the channels of the manifestation of God's Power. But it is true, however, that in the realm of Spiritual Power of the Almighty God, all men are not on the same level.

Our Lord Jesus Christ made it clear that in the Kingdom of God, in the highest realm of Spiritual Power, the children of God are established and operate on various degrees, such as thirty, sixty and hundred. **(See Math. 13:23)**

This shows that there are different degrees of operation of the Power of God via His children. To this end, a believer on a higher degree of His Power, will be used by Him to perform a miracle which a believer on a lower degree of His Power will not accomplish. Nevertheless, even the lowest degree of the Power of God is greater than the greatest degree of the powers of darkness. For all the true children of God in diverse degrees live in the essence of the consummate Spirit of the Lord God Almighty, with whom all things are possible.

CHAPTER 9

SIGNS AND SIGNET OF POWER

"God also bearing them witness, both with signs and wonders, and with diverse miracles, and gifts of the Holy Ghost, according to his own will."
(Heb. 2:4).

QUESTION
In your book (THE GREATEST REVELATION OF OUR TIME), the Lord for the first time called you 'Harbinger of the Last Covenant.' And from that moment you bear this title. Some people think that this is a strange title for a man of God. What is the spiritual significance of this?

The word **'Harbinger'** should not be strange to anyone. You can check the meaning in your dictionary because it is an English word. Simply expressed: Harbinger is a forerunner or a sign of something that is to come. Every believer is a forerunner of the Kingdom of God. And I am fully aware, however, by His grace, of my call in this connection.

Behold I give unto you power

Now, my assignment as the Harbinger of the Last Covenant, is the making of God and not that of any man or church. This mission involves the utilization of a highly concentrated Power of the Godhead. This mission is very much on course. It is a call for me to partake in, and bear witness of, the greatest movement of the Holy Spirit in the world of man.

A NEW BEGINNING

Presently, about seventy percent of this great mission, which is set forth by the Holy Spirit and operated by Him, and which must operate whether with or without me, is to cleanse the Earth Planet for the greatest NEW BEGINNING that will soon come; and it will come even greater than the days of Noah.

This is the work of the Holy Spirit, when the earthman will turn and see the evils of Satan no more. This is very important. The Spirit of God is about to bring a drastic change in the world of man to the end that the children of men will witness His Power as never before known on Earth. The Lord will do this by His Power, and it will come to pass that all will bear witness of the coming of the Lord of Hosts. I am playing my own little part in the movement of the Holy Spirit in this regard. All believers are playing their parts also.

Signs and signet of power

In my role, however, the Lord is also using me to be actively involved in averting major devices looming out of the wilderness of the powers of darkness and heading towards the world of man, especially towards the path of Nigeria's destiny. For instance, the Lord brought me to the recognition that Nigeria has been spiritually chosen by Him to manifest the Highest Light, Dominion, Seat and Essence of the Holy Spirit on Earth. And by His grace, I also received the Power to speak for Him to this end.

There are many things I will not say now. But one thing is that He has already revealed the things that will happen in Nigeria and the rest of the world for several years to come. And the spiritual key of the Holy Spirit is with me in this regard. This key is also with you if you are of Him.

THE REALITY OF GOD'S POWER

QUESTION
Some people doubt the reality of God's Power. Some people want to see before they believe. Do you think that God has sent you to prove the reality of His Power?

First of all, anyone who does not recognize the reality

of the Power of God is like a fish in the sea that denies the existence of water. Let me tell you this: we all experience the Power of God, whether we believe it or not, through our individual existence. Your daily existence is sustained by the Power of God; thus you experience God daily, whether you know it or not, through your existence. To this end, your life, which is sustained daily by the Living God, is the first evidence of the reality of the Power of God.

Secondly, the Scripture is there to reveal the true Power of the Almighty God. And God has many of His Prophets today on Earth to still confirm and uphold the Power of Jehovah God and His Christ, even the Power of the Holy Spirit.

Now remember that it was on the strength of the Power of the Almighty Jehovah God that Prophet Elijah left the Earth Planet without death. The Power of God manifested in the form of a strange whirlwind with chariot and horses of fire, which took Elijah into the higher realms of God. **2nd Kings chapter 2 verse 11,** says:

> *"And it came to pass, as they still went on, and talked, that, behold, there appeared a chariot of fire, and horses of fire, and parted them both asunder; and Elijah went up by a whirlwind into heaven ".*

Signs and signet of power

This is the Supreme Power we are talking of. (As it was in the beginning, is now, and ever shall be - world without end). Have you seen what His Power can do? A man like Elijah lived in the world of man in the consummate essence of the Power of the Almighty God.

Remember Shadrach, Meshach and Abednego. These were true agents of the Most High God, who triumphed over the great fire of Nebuchadnezzar by the Power and the physical Divine Manifestation of the Lord of Hosts who appeared as the Son of God. They refused to bow down before the mighty idol of the Prince of Darkness, which king Nebuchadnezzar of Babylon made for the entire people. Nebuchadnezzar became highly exasperated and commanded that the children of God be cast into the fire. When this was done, did the Power of the Living God disappoint them? Not at all. When they were cast into the burning fire, the Power of God manifested, and the Lord of Hosts came to deliver them. At last Nebuchadnezzar was bamboozled whilst the children of God prevailed with the Power of their Lord. **(See Dan. 3: 19 - 30)**.

What about the Power that divided the great sea for the children of Israel to pass through? That is the Power of the Almighty God. Think about this Power. Just believe - have absolute and unquestionable confidence (FAITH) in Him. His Power has never and can never fail. Did He fail the children of Israel when they came before the sea? Think of this Power which physically divided the sea for the people of God.

> *"And Moses stretched out his hand over the sea; and the LORD caused the sea to go back by a strong east wind all that night, and made the sea dry land, and the waters were divided. And the children of Israel went into the midst of the sea upon dry ground: and the waters were a wall unto them on their right hand, and on their left"* (Exo. 14:21,22).

The problem of the earthman is lack of faith in the limitless Power of the God of gods, even the God of Moses. I worship at the feet of Jehovah God who manifested His Almighty Power through Moses.

Now have you read the Book of Esther in the Bible? If you have not read it, please do so and bear witness of the Power of God. There you will read about Haman, a great agent of darkness, who rose against the people of God. He was the foremost adviser to Ahasuerus, king of Persia and Media and was regarded as the second-in-command to the king.

Haman fought the people of God to the extent that he made gallows to hang Mordecai, the servant of God. The people of God set themselves to seek help from God through 72 hours fasting and praying. Consequently, the limitless Power of Jehovah God came down. Now listen

Signs and signet of power

to what happened at last: *"So they hanged Haman on the gallows that he had prepared for Mordecai...* **(Esth. 7:10)**. Read the Book of Esther and see what happened.

The Power of God is real, very real! This Power is Omnipresent. This Power is everywhere at all times managing the Universe. This Power is here now. Our Lord Jesus Christ is the consummate and total manifestation of this Power in the world of man. He came and died for the children of men. But after three days and three nights in the grave of gross matter, Jesus Christ transcended death and arose as the Lord of Hosts, as the ultimate demonstration of Spiritual Power in the physical system of existence.

The Highest Power of God is constantly in motion. This Power is multidimensional. The words of the living entities (creatures), including that of men and the angels, can not fully describe the multitudinous facets of the limitless Power of the Almighty God who created all things.

Consider the works of His hand: think of the Sun, the Moon and the Stars. Think of the Earth Planet and all the planets of the Universe; all are sustained in the space by the Power of the Almighty God. Think of the ocean and the mountains of the Earth; think of the earthmen, the angels, mighty spirits of the realms beyond and the great living creatures in Heaven; think of the beasts of the Earth, the little creatures and the birds of the air. What of

Behold I give unto you power

the great things and mighty creatures unknown to the earthmen? All were created by the same Supreme Power which appeared in human form and known to us as Jesus Christ.

> *"All things were made by him; and without him was not anything made that was made.... He was in the world, and the world was made by him, and the world knew him not"* (John 1:3,10).

There is nothing that His Power can not do. Remember also that it was this very Power that caused lions to bow at the feet of Daniel, the Prophet of God: **(See Dan. 6).** By this very Power Elisha spoke and wild beast came out to kill and maim. **(See 2 Kings 2:24).** This is the same Power which Christ gave us to tread on all the powers of darkness.

OPERATIONS OF HIS POWER

QUESTION

Can you tell us how the Power of God operates through you. In other words, do you have a special way of attending to people who come to you with diverse needs, seeking the help of God?

Signs and signet of power

First of all, I am fully aware that I have no ability, wisdom, or power of my own. I depend solely on my Lord who is the Supreme Source of endless wisdom, ability and Power. To this end, I have no other 'special way' of attending to people other than to adhere strictly to the principles of Jehovah God and His Christ. Consequently, these principles are in two major aspects. Firstly, the Scripture (the Written Word of God) is my general guide on how to attend to the needs and problems of the earthmen.

Every true believer must uphold this principle. Secondly, the Word spoken or given to me directly by the Lord or His Angels, is my specific guide in this regard. This is very important, because I have to hear from the Lord before attending to difficult situations. If the Lord did not speak, then I can do nothing. And when He speaks, that is the final - it must stand or come to pass!

For instance, one day an army officer came to me to seek the blessings of the Lord. He was then a Colonel and Principal Staff Officer (PSO) of the National War College. He wanted God to do two things for him. As at then he learnt from a reliable source that he was about to be sent to the National Institute of Policy and Strategic Studies (N.I.P.S.S) Kuru, near Jos, from there to undue retirement. But this was not yet officially confirmed. Therefore he wanted the Lord to retain him at the War College as well as to grant him promotion. He believed in the Words of the Lord which has it that:

Behold I give unto you power

> *"The LORD maketh poor, and maketh rich: he bringeth low, and lifted up"*
> (1 Sam. 2:7).

> *"For promotion cometh neither from the east, nor from the west, nor from the south. But God is the judge: He putteth down one, and setteth up another"* (Psm. 75:6,7).

That same day I prayed unto the Lord my God for the officer. I prayed for him based on the Words of God in the Scriptures. However, there was no specific Word given to me by the Lord for him. But based on the written Words of Jesus Christ, I told him to go that all is well. Based on this also, I further told him to still give thanks to God for whatever happens on this matter in the final analysis.

It was already night whilst I told the officer to still see me in the morning by 9am the following day. I wanted to pray more to the Lord in my own private moment, with the thought that the Lord may finally speak to me concerning his matter. And while I was praying around the mid-night, the Word of God came to me, and He said:

> *"Son of man, behold, thou art My Harbinger and Prophet of your time. The key of My Power, O son of man, is with thee; for thou art set forth to fulfill the desires of My people..."*

Signs and signet of power

He said many other things to me that same moment. He specifically directed me to make a spiritual decree for the matter of the officer, by the Power of the Seven Spirits of the Living God; that he will not be transferred to Kuru; and that his promotion will surely come to pass at the War College before the end of three months from that moment; and that he will come into the high command of the Nigerian Army, even in the mighty name of the Lord Jesus Christ. Consequently, the following day, I made the spiritual decree upon the officer as ordained by the Lord. I simply anointed him, laid hands on him and pronounced the specific Words of the Lord upon him.

Some days after this, he received an official letter directing him to move down to Kuru with other officers sent there for a course. He went to Kuru as directed, thinking that the decree of the Lord through his messenger had failed. But the decree of the Lord can never fail in all realms of existence. If a Prophet speaks out of his volition, and not by the Spirit of God, it will fail. But if the Lord speaks through his Prophet, it must stand. **(See Isa. 55:10, 11 and Deut. 18:21, 22).**

The official letter that he should go to Kuru got to him because the letter was on the way to him even at the time that the Lord made the decree through me. But when he finally got to Kuru, he discovered that his name did not appear in the official list of those sent for the course there. Thus the officials of N.I.P.S.S., Kuru, told him that

Behold I give unto you power

he was not one of those sent to them, that he should please return and sort out things at the head-quarters.

The brother returned and went to the headquarters to sort out things. It was there he got to know that he has been promoted to Brig-Gen. by the Commander-in-Chief. He was also directed not to go to Kuru again but should remain where he was at the war college till further notice, according to the Word of the Lord, which I spoke to him. Then the brother rejoiced and praised the Lord. When Gods speaks, it must come to pass, only believe! This officer, Yellow Duke, finally retired from the army as Major-Gen. and Chief of Operations, Nigerian Army.

DIVINE PROVISION

Therefore as much as possible I have to receive from God first before making a specific decree or taking a specific or categorical stand on any matter brought to me by any person. I remember once I was ministering at Aba, Nigeria, and a sister came to me with a specific request to the Lord. Then I was ministering at the Pentecostal Power Mission, at 3 Umuagbal street, off Portharcourt Road, Aba . And the sister that came to me, sister Grace, is the wife of the founder of the church, then Rev. Abraham Akatuba, but now Rev. Abraham Ovie.

Signs and signet of power

This daughter of God told me categorically that she wants the Lord to provide her a car for the success of the work of the Lord. As at that moment she had only ten thousand naira (10,00,00) of her own whilst it will take about five hundred thousand naira for her to buy a used car. She believed in God, not in the mortal man, hence she came to seek the help of God.

I asked her, **"sister are you prepared to obey the principle of doing His work first and He will do yours?"** She said she was ready to do so. I asked her again whether she was prepared to give all that money as offering. She replied that she was prepared to obey. I then told her to go first and bring all her money to God and drop it at the feet His Messenger. This was the same principle which was used by Elijah the Prophet to bring testimony to the widow of Zarephath **(see 1kings 17:8-16)**. Sister Grace went and brought all her money to the Lord. Before I prayed for her, the Word of God came to me, saying:

> *"O ye Harbinger of the Last Covenant, verily the request of My Daughter Grace is granted. Now Speak to her and say, behold, from the inception of the offering of all you have, even of all your money, thus says the Lord, surely eight weeks shall not pass and your car will come, and thou shall glorify Me thy Lord"!*

Behold I give unto you power

At this point I called her husband and some Pastors to come out and bear me witness of what the Lord has said which must come to pass. Then I proclaimed the Word of God upon our sister. And it came to pass on the seventh week that sister Grace bought a new car as spoken by the Lord. It was a miracle, for the Power of the Lord opened a way for her where there was no way before; divine favor came forth and money came beyond her expectation.

Remember, with the Power of God, with the Spirit of God, all things are possible. The Supreme Power of the Almighty God operates in unlimited dimensions for our physical and spiritual progress. Just believe in Him and all is well. The most vital spiritual fact is that you must have faith in God. This is first step to the realm of His Power.

> *"And Jesus answering saith unto them, have faith in God. For verily I say unto you, that whosoever shall say unto this mountain, be thou removed, and be thou cast into the sea; and shall not doubt in his heart, but shall believe that those things which he saith shall come to pass; he shall have whatsoever he saith. Therefore I say unto you, what things so ever ye desire, when ye pray, believe that you receive them, and ye shall have them".*
>
> **(Mark 11:22-24)**

CHAPTER 10

HOW TO BE FIRM IN POWER

"Strengthened with all might, according to His glorious power, with joyfulness."
(Col.1:11).

QUESTION
Speaking strictly from the Holy Scriptures, how can one be victorious through the Power of the Almighty God?

FAITH AND CONSTANT PRAYER

First of all, the believer's faith in the victorious Christ and Lord of the Universe will assure him of the daily victorious Power of the Lord God Almighty. If one does not have the Spirit of Christ in the centre of his life, he is not assured of the victory of God's Power **(See John 3 : 14-21)**.

If we want to be victorious through the Power of God, we must follow the path of Jesus Christ, and following the path of Jesus Christ means living like Christ. Whosoever wants to live in the essence of the Holy Spirit must pray like Jesus Christ. This is very

important. Consider the life and works of Christ in this regard:

> *"And in the morning, rising up a great while before day, he went out, and departed into a solitary place, and there prayed"* **(Mark 1 : 35)**.

> *"And he spake a parable unto them to this end, that men ought always to pray and not to faint"* **(Luke 18:1)**.

MEDITATE ON GOD'S WORD

If we want to be victorious in the field of spiritual warfare, then it is imperative also that we meditate on God's Word on daily basis. Remember that the Word of God is Power. His Word is the sure foundation - the rock upon which we stand. Daily meditation on the Word of God puts us on the platform of consistent watchfulness. *"Watch and pray, that ye enter not into temptation..."* **(Matt. 26 : 41)**.

While meditating on the Word of the Lord, we must believe, we must have faith in His Word, otherwise our meditation is invalid. A true believer can not live without faith. We have to remember the Lord our God always with faith and meditate daily upon His Word. The Scripture admonished:

> *"This book of the law shall not depart out of thy mouth; but thou shalt meditate therein day and night, that thou mayest observe to do according to all that is written therein: for then thou shalt make thy way prosperous, and then thou shalt have good success"* **(Joshua 1: 8)**.

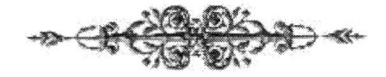

HAVE THE SPIRIT OF CHRIST

I have already said that if you want true Power, you must accept Christ into your life, you must be ruled by the everlasting Spirit of Our Lord Jesus Christ. No matter your level in the church circle, without definite conversion by the Spirit of Christ you can not possess the Spiritual Power of victory. If you doubt your salvation, then you have failed. But if your salvation is sure, then another thing that is very important is your early morning quiet-time with the Lord. It is written:

Behold I give unto you power

"O God, thou art my God; early will I seek thee: my soul thirsteth for thee, my flesh longeth for thee in a dry and thirsty land, where no water is". **(Psalm 63:1).**

Some so-called **'old Christians'** behave as if quiet time or seeking the Lord early in the morning is for new converts. Some people wake up in the morning and pray briefly, for few minutes, and then begin the day's job. This is not quiet-time. Quiet-time is to speak deeply to God and God speaks to you through His Scripture and much more, as well as to take time and pray the Word of God into your innermost spiritual being.

During your quiet-time in the morning, take time to praise the Lord your God, read your Bible and pray. Don't wake up and say few words of prayer just to clear your conscience that you have prayed after all. Remember, your general spiritual victory throughout the day depends largely on your degree of communication with God early in the morning.

It is important that we spend not less than one hour fully with the Lord each morning. But some of us spend between ten to fifteen minutes and jump out. When you spend time and settle with the Holy Spirit in the morning, you are placed on the path of victory throughout the day. Of course every true believer knows the importance of quiet-time, but some of us are lazy to do so.

How to be firm in power

A true child of God must pray always to the Lord His God - morning, afternoon, night, all the time. Your prayer life reveals the degree on which you depend in God. We can do nothing without the Word of God. The Word of God is the source of all things, which the Lord has even magnified above His name

> *"I will worship toward thy holy temple, and praise thy name for thy lovingkindness and for thy truth: for thou hast magnified thy word above all thy name".* **(Psm. 138:2).**

Victorious spiritual life is not by magic. You have to plan for it, pray for it and work towards it. Are you a **"believer"** who worships only on Sundays without taking part in the weekly activities and fellowship in the 'House of God?' I tell you the truth, anything that takes you away from regular fellowship among the people of God, is capable of taking you away from the Kingdom of God.

ABOVE DARK POWERS

QUESTION
Considering your former position in the world of darkness, there is no doubt that the forces of

darkness will look at you as a major target of their spiritual attack. Can you tell us a little about this attack and how the Power of God has been seeing you through?

First of all, I want to say that I did not call myself. I was directly called into the path of Light by the Lord Himself. And because Our Lord Jesus Christ is the Sole Ultimate Power in the Universe, I am confident that He will always fight and conquer for me. My protection is in His hands, therefore the powers of darkness can do me nothing. This is the true situation. I am above the powers of darkness.

It is true that the powers of darkness have been trying their games against me, but they can do me nothing as far as the Power of Christ is with me. My concern is not what the powers of darkness can do, but that I may remain faithful to the Lord. For as long as one remains faithful, true and worthy to the Lord, nothing in the Universe will harm him. The Scriptures says:

> *"No weapon that is formed against thee shall prosper; and every tongue that shall rise against thee in judgment thou shalt condemn. This is the heritage of the servants of the LORD, and their righteousness is of me, saith the LORD"*
> (Isa. 54 : 17)

So my heritage and portion in the Lord is daily victory over all the manipulations of the Prince of Darkness. And, of course, my righteousness is of the Lord and not of any person or group of persons. The same with the righteousness and heritage of all the servants of God (past and present). I am aware, however, of how the powers of darkness possessed some people and used them to fight me through vicious campaigns of calumny and false propaganda, that I have gone back into the occult; that I have gone mad, and much more. But all these matter nothing to me. I am a Prophet of God by His special grace. And anyone on this path must face the false propaganda of the Prince of Darkness co-ordinated by the faithless, the hypocrites, the imbeciles and the false shepherds.

QUESTION
You are fully convinced that in Christ your victory and protection is sure?

Every child of God should be convinced of this. Christ is the Power above powers, and whosoever is in Him is free and free indeed. Darkness flees from the Light, therefore the powers of darkness must flee from each and every child of Christ, the Supreme Light.

QUESTION
Finally what is your advice to the Hearers of this message?

I say, let them rise in the strength of the Spirit of God and overcome all that comes from the realm of darkness, through Jesus Christ Our Lord

- Amen.

BOOKS BY IYKE NATHAN UZORMA

1. OCCULT GRAND MASTER NOW IN CHRIST - *Vol. 1*
2. EXPOSING THE RULERS OF DARKNESS *(In recognition of the highest power) Vol. 1*
3. THE SPIRIT REALM *Vol. 1*
4. OVERCOMING THE FORCES AGAINST SUCCESSFUL MARRIAGE
5. EXPOSING THE RULERS OF DARKNESS *(In recognition of the highest power) Vol. 2*
6. POWERS FOR PULLING DOWN THE CONTROLLING FORCES OF DARKNESS
7. THE PATH OF PERFECTION - *Vol. 1*
8. THE GRAND PLAN TO DESTROY NIGERIA
9. THE OCCULTIC STRONGHOLDS IN NIGERIA AND THE REST OF THE WORLD
10. LYING SPIRIT OF THE OCCULT - *Vol. 1*
11. THE GREATEST REVELATION OF OUR TIME. - *Vol. 1*
12. WORLD-WIDE SPIRITUAL BATTLE IN NIGERIA BEFORE AND BEYOND ABACHA
13. FORMER OCCULT GRAND MASTER NOW IN CHRIST SPEAKS
14. HOW TO COMPLETELY OVERCOME WITCHES AND WIZARDS AND ALL THE POWERS OF DARKNESS
15. THE SEVEN CYCLES OF SPIRITUAL ATTACK ON BUSINESS *(Exposed on earth for the first time)*
16. TOWARDS THE REIGN OF RIGHTEOUSNESS
17. BEHOLD I GIVE UNTO YOU POWER
18. HUMAN RIGHTS ABUSE IN THE LIGHT OF REALITY
19. KNOW YOUR ENEMIES WATCH YOUR FRIENDS

BOOKS BY IYKE NATHAN UZORMA

20. THE SPIRIT REALM *Vol. 2*
21. SECRETS FROM HEAVEN
22. THE GREATEST EVIDENCE OF GOD'S POWER IN OUR TIME
23. OCCULT GRAND MASTER NOW IN CHRIST - *Vol. 2*
24. OCCULT GRAND MASTER NOW IN CHRIST - *Vol. 3*
25. PARADOX OF EXISTENCE
26. THE GREATEST STRANGE BEING NOW ON EARTH
27. THE FUTURE EARTH
28. MY 300 MINUTES EXPERIENCE OF HEAVEN
29. THE BOOK OF TESTIMONIES - *Vol. 1*
30. THOU SHALL DECREE A THING
31. THE BOOK OF LIGHT
32. DEEPER REALITIES OF EXISTENCE *Vol.1*
33. HIDDEN TRUTH OF MAN AND WOMAN
34. THE PATH PERFECTION *Vol.2*
35. EARTHMEN RETURN TO THYSELF
36. THE KINGDOM OF GOD IS WITHIN YOU

AND OTHERS

New Book By
Iyke Nathan Uzorma

The Seven Cycles Of Spiritual Attack On Business

Exposed For The First Time On Earth

THE SEVEN CYCLES SPIRITUAL ATTACK & Business

SPECIAL REVISED EDITION

With A Specific Divine Revelation On How Your Finance Will Rise Beyond All Systems And Cycles Of The Astral Psychic Attack

IYKE NATHAN UZORMA

TO OBTAIN
THIS BOOK BY SPECIAL ORDER,
WITH A FREEWILL DONATION,
CALL: +234-(0)8052795749

New Book By
Iyke Nathan Uzorma
DEEPER REALITIES OF EXISTENCE

Deeper Realities of Existence, is a book that holds for mankind a message of profound truth and revelation of hidden mysteries. It is the panacea to all forms of physical, psychological and psychic terrorism, including vicious Astral attack. This book elucidates the basis of Planetary Winnowing in this Age, the core terrestrial and extraterrestrial danger of atomic radiation unknown to mundane scientists, Universal Signet of the Supreme Mastership of Christ, Immutable Laws of the Universe, the rise of a sane civilization of Universal Brotherhood on Earth, amongst others.

Notes

Notes

Printed in Great Britain
by Amazon